The Book of
Psalms

New American Standard

LARGE PRINT

entirely JESUS

Published by Entirely Jesus
Entirelyjesus.com

Compiled by and Cover Design by: P.A. Austen
Cover Painting by William Kay Blacklock (1872-1922),
"The Shepherd's Daughter"

ISBN-10: 1-948229-10-2
ISBN-13: 978-1-948229-10-4

Print, Softcover, First Edition, Large Print
Tennessee, United States of America

Psalm and Page Number

Psalm 1

1. How blessed is the man who does not walk
in the counsel of the wicked,
>   Nor stand in the path of sinners,
>   Nor sit in the seat of scoffers!

2. But his delight is in the law of the LORD,
>   And in His law he meditates day and
night.

3. He will be like a tree firmly planted by
streams of water,
>   Which yields its fruit in its season
>   And its leaf does not wither;
>   And in whatever he does, he prospers.

4. The wicked are not so,
>   But they are like chaff which the wind
drives away.

5. Therefore the wicked will not stand in the
judgment,
>   Nor sinners in the assembly of the
righteous.

6. For the LORD knows the way of the righteous,
>   But the way of the wicked will perish.

Psalm 2

1. Why are the nations in an uproar
>   And the peoples devising a vain thing?

2. The kings of the earth take their stand,
>   And the rulers take counsel together
>   Against the LORD and against His Anointed, saying,

3. "Let us tear their fetters apart
>   And cast away their cords from us!"

4. He who sits in the heavens laughs,
>   The Lord scoffs at them.

5. Then He will speak to them in His anger
>   And terrify them in His fury, saying,

6. "But as for Me, I have installed My King
>   Upon Zion, My holy mountain."

7. "I will surely tell of the decree of the LORD:
     He said to Me, 'You are My Son,
     Today I have begotten You.

8. 'Ask of Me, and I will surely give the nations
as Your inheritance,
     And the very ends of the earth as Your
possession.

9. 'You shall break them with a rod of iron,
     You shall shatter them like
earthenware.'"

10. Now therefore, O kings, show discernment;
     Take warning, O judges of the earth.

11. Worship the LORD with reverence
     And rejoice with trembling.

12. Do homage to the Son, that He not become
angry, and you perish in the way,
     For His wrath may soon be kindled.
     How blessed are all who take refuge in
Him!

Psalm 3

1. O LORD, how my adversaries have
increased!
> Many are rising up against me.

2. Many are saying of my soul,
> "There is no deliverance for him in
God."

3. But You, O LORD, are a shield about me,
> My glory, and the One who lifts my
head.

4. I was crying to the LORD with my voice,
> And He answered me from His holy
mountain.

5. I lay down and slept;
> I awoke, for the LORD sustains me.

6. I will not be afraid of ten thousands of people
> Who have set themselves against me
round about.

7. Arise, O LORD; save me, O my God!
> For You have smitten all my enemies on
the cheek;

You have shattered the teeth of the
wicked.

8. Salvation belongs to the LORD;
 Your blessing be upon Your people!

Psalm 4

1. Answer me when I call, O God of my
righteousness!
 You have relieved me in my distress;
 Be gracious to me and hear my prayer.

2. O sons of men, how long will my honor
become a reproach?
 How long will you love what is
worthless and aim at deception?

3. But know that the LORD has set apart the
godly man for Himself;
 The LORD hears when I call to Him.

4. Tremble, and do not sin;
 Meditate in your heart upon your bed,
and be still.

5. Offer the sacrifices of righteousness,
> And trust in the LORD.

6. Many are saying, "Who will show us any good?"
> Lift up the light of Your countenance upon us, O LORD!

7. You have put gladness in my heart,
> More than when their grain and new wine abound.

8. In peace I will both lie down and sleep,
> For You alone, O LORD, make me to dwell in safety.

Psalm 5

1. Give ear to my words, O LORD,
> Consider my groaning.

2. Heed the sound of my cry for help, my King and my God,
> For to You I pray.

3. In the morning, O LORD, You will hear my voice;

In the morning I will order my prayer to You and eagerly watch.

4. For You are not a God who takes pleasure in wickedness;
  No evil dwells with You.

5. The boastful shall not stand before Your eyes;
  You hate all who do iniquity.

6. You destroy those who speak falsehood;
  The LORD abhors the man of bloodshed and deceit.

7. But as for me, by Your abundant lovingkindness I will enter Your house,
  At Your holy temple I will bow in reverence for You.

8. O LORD, lead me in Your righteousness because of my foes;
  Make Your way straight before me.

9. There is nothing reliable in what they say;
  Their inward part is destruction itself.
  Their throat is an open grave;
  They flatter with their tongue.

10. Hold them guilty, O God;
    By their own devices let them fall!
    In the multitude of their transgressions
thrust them out,
    For they are rebellious against You.

11. But let all who take refuge in You be glad,
    Let them ever sing for joy;
    And may You shelter them,
    That those who love Your name may
exult in You.

12. For it is You who blesses the righteous man,
O LORD,
    You surround him with favor as with a
shield.

1. O LORD, do not rebuke me in Your anger,
    Nor chasten me in Your wrath.

2. Be gracious to me, O LORD, for I am pining
away;
    Heal me, O LORD, for my bones are
dismayed.

3. And my soul is greatly dismayed;
    But You, O LORD—how long?

4. Return, O LORD, rescue my soul;
    Save me because of Your
lovingkindness.

5. For there is no mention of You in death;
    In Sheol, who will give You thanks?

6. I am weary with my sighing;
    Every night I make my bed swim,
    I dissolve my couch with my tears.

7. My eye has wasted away with grief;
    It has become old because of all my
adversaries.

8. Depart from me, all you who do iniquity,
    For the LORD has heard the voice of my
weeping.

9. The LORD has heard my supplication,
    The LORD receives my prayer.

10. All my enemies will be ashamed and
greatly dismayed;
    They shall turn back, they will suddenly
be ashamed.

Psalm 7

1. O LORD my God, in You I have taken refuge;
>   Save me from all those who pursue me, and deliver me,

2. Or he will tear my soul like a lion,
>   Dragging me away, while there is none to deliver.

3. O LORD my God, if I have done this,
>   If there is injustice in my hands,

4. If I have rewarded evil to my friend,
>   Or have plundered him who without cause was my adversary,

5. Let the enemy pursue my soul and overtake it;
>   And let him trample my life down to the ground
>   And lay my glory in the dust.

6. Arise, O LORD, in Your anger;
>   Lift up Yourself against the rage of my adversaries,

And arouse Yourself for me; You have
appointed judgment.

7. Let the assembly of the peoples encompass
You,
> And over them return on high.

8. The LORD judges the peoples;
> Vindicate me, O LORD, according to my
righteousness and my integrity that is in me.

9. O let the evil of the wicked come to an end,
but establish the righteous;
> For the righteous God tries the hearts
and minds.

10. My shield is with God,
> Who saves the upright in heart.

11. God is a righteous judge,
> And a God who has indignation every
day.

12. If a man does not repent, He will sharpen
His sword;
> He has bent His bow and made it ready.

13. He has also prepared for Himself deadly weapons;

> He makes His arrows fiery shafts.

14. Behold, he travails with wickedness,

> And he conceives mischief and brings forth falsehood.

15. He has dug a pit and hollowed it out,

> And has fallen into the hole which he made.

16. His mischief will return upon his own head,

> And his violence will descend upon his own pate.

17. I will give thanks to the LORD according to His righteousness,

> And I will sing praise to the name of the LORD Most High.

Psalm 8

1. O LORD, our Lord,
    How majestic is Your name in all the
earth,
    You have displayed Your splendor
above the heavens!

2. From the mouth of infants and nursing
babes, You have established strength,
    Because of Your adversaries,
    To make the enemy and the revengeful
cease.

3. When I consider Your heavens, the work of
Your fingers,
    The moon and the stars, which You have
ordained;

4. What is man that You take thought of him,
    And the son of man that You care for
him?

5. Yet You have made him a little lower than
God,
    And You crown him with glory and
majesty!

6. You make him to rule over the works of Your hands;
> You have put all things under his feet,

7. All sheep and oxen,
> And also the beasts of the field,

8. The birds of the heavens and the fish of the sea,
> Whatever passes through the paths of the seas.

9. O LORD, our Lord,
> How majestic is Your name in all the earth!

Psalm 9

1. I will give thanks to the LORD with all my heart;
> I will tell of all Your wonders.

2. I will be glad and exult in You;
> I will sing praise to Your name, O Most High.

3. When my enemies turn back,
> They stumble and perish before You.

4. For You have maintained my just cause;
   You have sat on the throne judging
righteously.

5. You have rebuked the nations, You have
destroyed the wicked;
   You have blotted out their name forever
and ever.

6. The enemy has come to an end in perpetual
ruins,
   And You have uprooted the cities;
   The very memory of them has perished.

7. But the LORD abides forever;
   He has established His throne for
judgment,

8. And He will judge the world in
righteousness;
   He will execute judgment for the
peoples with equity.

9. The LORD also will be a stronghold for the
oppressed,
   A stronghold in times of trouble;

10. And those who know Your name will put their trust in You,

    For You, O LORD, have not forsaken those who seek You.

11. Sing praises to the LORD, who dwells in Zion;

    Declare among the peoples His deeds.

12. For He who requires blood remembers them;

    He does not forget the cry of the afflicted.

13. Be gracious to me, O LORD;

    See my affliction from those who hate me,

    You who lift me up from the gates of death,

14. That I may tell of all Your praises,

    That in the gates of the daughter of Zion
    I may rejoice in Your salvation.

15. The nations have sunk down in the pit which they have made;

    In the net which they hid, their own foot has been caught.

16. The LORD has made Himself known;
	He has executed judgment.
	In the work of his own hands the wicked
is snared.

17. The wicked will return to Sheol,
	Even all the nations who forget God.

18. For the needy will not always be forgotten,
	Nor the hope of the afflicted perish
forever.

19. Arise, O LORD, do not let man prevail;
	Let the nations be judged before You.

20. Put them in fear, O LORD;
	Let the nations know that they are but
men.

<u>Psalm 10</u>

1. Why do You stand afar off, O LORD?
	Why do You hide Yourself in times of
trouble?

2. In pride the wicked hotly pursue the
afflicted;

Let them be caught in the plots which they have devised.

3. For the wicked boasts of his heart's desire,
    And the greedy man curses and spurns the LORD.

4. The wicked, in the haughtiness of his countenance, does not seek Him.
    All his thoughts are, "There is no God."

5. His ways prosper at all times;
    Your judgments are on high, out of his sight;
    As for all his adversaries, he snorts at them.

6. He says to himself, "I will not be moved;
    Throughout all generations I will not be in adversity."

7. His mouth is full of curses and deceit and oppression;
    Under his tongue is mischief and wickedness.

8. He sits in the lurking places of the villages;
    In the hiding places he kills the innocent;

His eyes stealthily watch for the unfortunate.

9. He lurks in a hiding place as a lion in his lair;
> He lurks to catch the afflicted;
> He catches the afflicted when he draws
him into his net.

10. He crouches, he bows down,
> And the unfortunate fall by his mighty
ones.

11. He says to himself, "God has forgotten;
> He has hidden His face; He will never
see it."

12. Arise, O LORD; O God, lift up Your hand.
> Do not forget the afflicted.

13. Why has the wicked spurned God?
> He has said to himself, "You will not
require it."

14. You have seen it, for You have beheld
mischief and vexation to take it into Your hand.
> The unfortunate commits himself to
You;
> You have been the helper of the orphan.

15. Break the arm of the wicked and the evildoer,
> Seek out his wickedness until You find none.

16. The LORD is King forever and ever;
> Nations have perished from His land.

17. O LORD, You have heard the desire of the humble;
> You will strengthen their heart; You will incline Your ear

18. To vindicate the orphan and the oppressed,
> So that man who is of the earth will no longer cause terror.

Psalm 11

1. In the LORD I take refuge;
> How can you say to my soul, "Flee as a bird to your mountain;"

2. For, behold, the wicked bend the bow,
> They make ready their arrow upon the string

To shoot in darkness at the upright in heart.

3. If the foundations are destroyed,
   What can the righteous do?

4. The LORD is in His holy temple; the LORD'S throne is in heaven;
   His eyes behold, His eyelids test the sons of men.

5. The LORD tests the righteous and the wicked,
   And the one who loves violence His soul hates.

6. Upon the wicked He will rain snares;
   Fire and brimstone and burning wind will be the portion of their cup.

7. For the LORD is righteous, He loves righteousness;
   The upright will behold His face.

Psalm 12

1. Help, LORD, for the godly man ceases to be,
      For the faithful disappear from among
the sons of men.

2. They speak falsehood to one another;
      With flattering lips and with a double
heart they speak.

3. May the LORD cut off all flattering lips,
      The tongue that speaks great things;

4. Who have said, "With our tongue we will
prevail;
      Our lips are our own; who is lord over
us?"

5. "Because of the devastation of the afflicted,
because of the groaning of the needy,
      Now I will arise," says the LORD; "I will
set him in the safety for which he longs."

6. The words of the LORD are pure words;
      As silver tried in a furnace on the earth,
refined seven times.

7. You, O LORD, will keep them;
        You will preserve him from this
generation forever.

8. The wicked strut about on every side
        When vileness is exalted among the sons
of men.

Psalm 13

1. How long, O LORD? Will You forget me
forever?
        How long will You hide Your face from
me?

2. How long shall I take counsel in my soul,
        Having sorrow in my heart all the day?
        How long will my enemy be exalted
over me?

3. Consider and answer me, O LORD my God;
        Enlighten my eyes, or I will sleep the
sleep of death,

4. And my enemy will say, "I have overcome
him,"
        And my adversaries will rejoice when I
am shaken.

5. But I have trusted in Your lovingkindness;
　　My heart shall rejoice in Your salvation.

6. I will sing to the LORD,
　　Because He has dealt bountifully with
me.

Psalm 14

1. The fool has said in his heart, "There is no
God."
　　They are corrupt, they have committed
abominable deeds;
　　There is no one who does good.

2. The LORD has looked down from heaven
upon the sons of men
　　To see if there are any who understand,
　　Who seek after God.

3. They have all turned aside, together they
have become corrupt;
　　There is no one who does good, not even
one.

4. Do all the workers of wickedness not know,
　　Who eat up my people as they eat bread,
　　And do not call upon the Lord?

5. There they are in great dread,
	For God is with the righteous generation.

6. You would put to shame the counsel of the afflicted,
	But the LORD is his refuge.

7. Oh, that the salvation of Israel would come out of Zion!
	When the LORD restores His captive people,
	Jacob will rejoice, Israel will be glad.

Psalm 15

1. O LORD, who may abide in Your tent?
	Who may dwell on Your holy hill?

2. He who walks with integrity, and works righteousness,
	And speaks truth in his heart.

3. He does not slander with his tongue,
	Nor does evil to his neighbor,
	Nor takes up a reproach against his friend;

4. In whose eyes a reprobate is despised,
    But who honors those who fear the
LORD;
    He swears to his own hurt and does not
change;

5. He does not put out his money at interest,
    Nor does he take a bribe against the
innocent.
    He who does these things will never be
shaken.

Psalm 16

1. Preserve me, O God, for I take refuge in You.

2. I said to the LORD, "You are my Lord;
    I have no good besides You."

3. As for the saints who are in the earth,
    They are the majestic ones in whom is all
my delight.

4. The sorrows of those who have bartered for
another god will be multiplied;
    I shall not pour out their drink offerings
of blood,

Nor will I take their names upon my lips.

5. The LORD is the portion of my inheritance and my cup;
    You support my lot.

6. The lines have fallen to me in pleasant places;
    Indeed, my heritage is beautiful to me.

7. I will bless the LORD who has counseled me;
    Indeed, my mind instructs me in the night.

8. I have set the LORD continually before me;
    Because He is at my right hand, I will not be shaken.

9. Therefore my heart is glad and my glory rejoices;
    My flesh also will dwell securely.

10. For You will not abandon my soul to Sheol;
    Nor will You allow Your Holy One to undergo decay.

11. You will make known to me the path of life;
    In Your presence is fullness of joy;

In Your right hand there are pleasures forever.

Psalm 17

1. Hear a just cause, O LORD, give heed to my cry;
Give ear to my prayer, which is not from deceitful lips.

2. Let my judgment come forth from Your presence;
Let Your eyes look with equity.

3. You have tried my heart;
You have visited me by night;
You have tested me and You find nothing;
I have purposed that my mouth will not transgress.

4. As for the deeds of men, by the word of Your lips
I have kept from the paths of the violent.

5. My steps have held fast to Your paths.
My feet have not slipped.

6. I have called upon You, for You will answer me, O God;

> Incline Your ear to me, hear my speech.

7. Wondrously show Your lovingkindness,

> O Savior of those who take refuge at
Your right hand

> From those who rise up against them.

8. Keep me as the apple of the eye;

> Hide me in the shadow of Your wings

9. From the wicked who despoil me,

> My deadly enemies who surround me.

10. They have closed their unfeeling heart,

> With their mouth they speak proudly.

11. They have now surrounded us in our steps;

> They set their eyes to cast us down to the
ground.

12. He is like a lion that is eager to tear,

> And as a young lion lurking in hiding
places.

13. Arise, O LORD, confront him, bring him low;

Deliver my soul from the wicked with Your sword,

14. From men with Your hand, O LORD,
From men of the world, whose portion is in this life,
And whose belly You fill with Your treasure;
They are satisfied with children,
And leave their abundance to their babes.

15. As for me, I shall behold Your face in righteousness;
I will be satisfied with Your likeness when I awake.

Psalm 18

1. "I love You, O LORD, my strength."

2. The LORD is my rock and my fortress and my deliverer,
My God, my rock, in whom I take refuge;
My shield and the horn of my salvation, my stronghold.

3. I call upon the LORD, who is worthy to be praised,

> And I am saved from my enemies.

4. The cords of death encompassed me,

> And the torrents of ungodliness terrified

me.

5. The cords of Sheol surrounded me;

> The snares of death confronted me.

6. In my distress I called upon the LORD,

> And cried to my God for help;
> He heard my voice out of His temple,
> And my cry for help before Him came

into His ears.

7. Then the earth shook and quaked;

> And the foundations of the mountains

were trembling

> And were shaken, because He was

angry.

8. Smoke went up out of His nostrils,

> And fire from His mouth devoured;
> Coals were kindled by it.

9. He bowed the heavens also, and came down
       With thick darkness under His feet.

10. He rode upon a cherub and flew;
       And He sped upon the wings of the
wind.

11. He made darkness His hiding place, His
canopy around Him,
       Darkness of waters, thick clouds of the
skies.

12. From the brightness before Him passed His
thick clouds,
       Hailstones and coals of fire.

13. The LORD also thundered in the heavens,
       And the Most High uttered His voice,
       Hailstones and coals of fire.

14. He sent out His arrows, and scattered them,
       And lightning flashes in abundance, and
routed them.

15. Then the channels of water appeared,
       And the foundations of the world were
laid bare
       At Your rebuke, O LORD,

At the blast of the breath of Your
nostrils.

16. He sent from on high, He took me;
       He drew me out of many waters.

17. He delivered me from my strong enemy,
       And from those who hated me, for they
were too mighty for me.

18. They confronted me in the day of my
calamity,
       But the LORD was my stay.

19. He brought me forth also into a broad place;
       He rescued me, because He delighted in
me.

20. The LORD has rewarded me according to
my righteousness;
       According to the cleanness of my hands
He has recompensed me.

21. For I have kept the ways of the LORD,
       And have not wickedly departed from
my God.

22. For all His ordinances were before me,
    And I did not put away His statutes
from me.

23. I was also blameless with Him,
    And I kept myself from my iniquity.

24. Therefore the LORD has recompensed me
according to my righteousness,
    According to the cleanness of my hands
in His eyes.

25. With the kind You show Yourself kind;
    With the blameless You show Yourself
blameless;

26. With the pure You show Yourself pure,
    And with the crooked You show
Yourself astute.

27. For You save an afflicted people,
    But haughty eyes You abase.

28. For You light my lamp;
    The LORD my God illumines my
darkness.

29. For by You I can run upon a troop;
    And by my God I can leap over a wall.

30. As for God, His way is blameless;
   The word of the LORD is tried;
   He is a shield to all who take refuge in Him.

31. For who is God, but the LORD?
   And who is a rock, except our God,

32. The God who girds me with strength
   And makes my way blameless?

33. He makes my feet like hinds' feet,
   And sets me upon my high places.

34. He trains my hands for battle,
   So that my arms can bend a bow of bronze.

35. You have also given me the shield of Your salvation,
   And Your right hand upholds me;
   And Your gentleness makes me great.

36. You enlarge my steps under me,
   And my feet have not slipped.

37. I pursued my enemies and overtook them,
   And I did not turn back until they were consumed.

38. I shattered them, so that they were not able to rise;
> They fell under my feet.

39. For You have girded me with strength for battle;
> You have subdued under me those who rose up against me.

40. You have also made my enemies turn their backs to me,
> And I destroyed those who hated me.

41. They cried for help, but there was none to save,
> Even to the LORD, but He did not answer them.

42. Then I beat them fine as the dust before the wind;
> I emptied them out as the mire of the streets.

43. You have delivered me from the contentions of the people;
> You have placed me as head of the nations;

A people whom I have not known serve
me.

44. As soon as they hear, they obey me;
    Foreigners submit to me.

45. Foreigners fade away,
    And come trembling out of their
fortresses.

46. The LORD lives, and blessed be my rock;
    And exalted be the God of my salvation,

47. The God who executes vengeance for me,
    And subdues peoples under me.

48. He delivers me from my enemies;
    Surely You lift me above those who rise
up against me;
    You rescue me from the violent man.

49. Therefore I will give thanks to You among
the nations, O LORD,
    And I will sing praises to Your name.

50. He gives great deliverance to His king,
    And shows lovingkindness to His
anointed,
    To David and his descendants forever.

Psalm 19

1. The heavens are telling of the glory of God;
    And their expanse is declaring the work
of His hands.

2. Day to day pours forth speech,
    And night to night reveals knowledge.

3. There is no speech, nor are there words;
    Their voice is not heard.

4. Their line has gone out through all the earth,
    And their utterances to the end of the
world.
    In them He has placed a tent for the sun,

5. Which is as a bridegroom coming out of his
chamber;
    It rejoices as a strong man to run his
course.

6. Its rising is from one end of the heavens,
    And its circuit to the other end of them;
    And there is nothing hidden from its
heat.

7. The law of the LORD is perfect, restoring the soul;

The testimony of the LORD is sure, making wise the simple.

8. The precepts of the LORD are right, rejoicing the heart;

The commandment of the LORD is pure, enlightening the eyes.

9. The fear of the LORD is clean, enduring forever;

The judgments of the LORD are true; they are righteous altogether.

10. They are more desirable than gold, yes, than much fine gold;

Sweeter also than honey and the drippings of the honeycomb.

11. Moreover, by them Your servant is warned; In keeping them there is great reward.

12. Who can discern his errors? Acquit me of hidden faults.

13. Also keep back Your servant from presumptuous sins;

Let them not rule over me;
Then I will be blameless,
And I shall be acquitted of great
transgression.

14. Let the words of my mouth and the
meditation of my heart
Be acceptable in Your sight,
O LORD, my rock and my Redeemer.

Psalm 20

1. May the LORD answer you in the day of
trouble!
May the name of the God of Jacob set
you securely on high!

2. May He send you help from the sanctuary
And support you from Zion!

3. May He remember all your meal offerings
And find your burnt offering acceptable!

4. May He grant you your heart's desire
And fulfill all your counsel!

5. We will sing for joy over your victory,
And in the name of our God we will set up our banners.
May the LORD fulfill all your petitions.

6. Now I know that the LORD saves His anointed;
He will answer him from His holy heaven
With the saving strength of His right hand.

7. Some boast in chariots and some in horses,
But we will boast in the name of the LORD, our God.

8. They have bowed down and fallen,
But we have risen and stood upright.

9. Save, O LORD;
May the King answer us in the day we call.

Psalm 21

1. O LORD, in Your strength the king will be glad,
>   And in Your salvation how greatly he will rejoice!

2. You have given him his heart's desire,
>   And You have not withheld the request of his lips.

3. For You meet him with the blessings of good things;
>   You set a crown of fine gold on his head.

4. He asked life of You,
>   You gave it to him,
>   Length of days forever and ever.

5. His glory is great through Your salvation,
>   Splendor and majesty You place upon him.

6. For You make him most blessed forever;
>   You make him joyful with gladness in Your presence.

7. For the king trusts in the LORD,
     And through the lovingkindness of the
Most High he will not be shaken.

8. Your hand will find out all your enemies;
     Your right hand will find out those who
hate you.

9. You will make them as a fiery oven in the
time of your anger;
     The LORD will swallow them up in His
wrath,
     And fire will devour them.

10. Their offspring You will destroy from the
earth,
     And their descendants from among the
sons of men.

11. Though they intended evil against You
          And devised a plot,
          They will not succeed.

12. For You will make them turn their back;
     You will aim with Your bowstrings at
their faces.

13. Be exalted, O LORD, in Your strength;
    We will sing and praise Your power.

Psalm 22

1. My God, my God, why have You forsaken me?
    Far from my deliverance are the words of my groaning.

2. O my God, I cry by day, but You do not answer;
    And by night, but I have no rest.

3. Yet You are holy,
    O You who are enthroned upon the praises of Israel.

4. In You our fathers trusted;
    They trusted and You delivered them.

5. To You they cried out and were delivered;
    In You they trusted and were not disappointed.

6. But I am a worm and not a man,
     A reproach of men and despised by the people.

7. All who see me sneer at me;
     They separate with the lip, they wag the head, saying,

8. "Commit yourself to the LORD; let Him deliver him;
     Let Him rescue him, because He delights in him."

9. Yet You are He who brought me forth from the womb;
     You made me trust when upon my mother's breasts.

10. Upon You I was cast from birth;
     You have been my God from my mother's womb.

11. Be not far from me, for trouble is near;
     For there is none to help.

12. Many bulls have surrounded me;
     Strong bulls of Bashan have encircled me.

13. They open wide their mouth at me,
     As a ravening and a roaring lion.

14. I am poured out like water,
     And all my bones are out of joint;
     My heart is like wax;
     It is melted within me.

15. My strength is dried up like a potsherd,
     And my tongue cleaves to my jaws;
     And You lay me in the dust of death.

16. For dogs have surrounded me;
     A band of evildoers has encompassed
me;
     They pierced my hands and my feet.

17. I can count all my bones.
     They look, they stare at me;

18. They divide my garments among them,
     And for my clothing they cast lots.

19. But You, O LORD, be not far off;
     O You my help, hasten to my assistance.

20. Deliver my soul from the sword,
     My only life from the power of the dog.

21. Save me from the lion's mouth;
     From the horns of the wild oxen You answer me.

22. I will tell of Your name to my brethren;
     In the midst of the assembly I will praise You.

23. You who fear the LORD, praise Him;
     All you descendants of Jacob, glorify Him,
     And stand in awe of Him, all you descendants of Israel.

24. For He has not despised nor abhorred the affliction of the afflicted;
     Nor has He hidden His face from him;
     But when he cried to Him for help, He heard.

25. From You comes my praise in the great assembly;
     I shall pay my vows before those who fear Him.

26. The afflicted will eat and be satisfied;
     Those who seek Him will praise the

LORD.

Let your heart live forever!

27. All the ends of the earth will remember and turn to the LORD,

And all the families of the nations will worship before You.

28. For the kingdom is the LORD'S

And He rules over the nations.

29. All the prosperous of the earth will eat and worship,

All those who go down to the dust will bow before Him,

Even he who cannot keep his soul alive.

30. Posterity will serve Him;

It will be told of the Lord to the coming generation.

31. They will come and will declare His righteousness

To a people who will be born, that He has performed it.

Psalm 23

1. The LORD is my shepherd,
    I shall not want.

2. He makes me lie down in green pastures;
    He leads me beside quiet waters.

3. He restores my soul;
    He guides me in the paths of
righteousness
    For His name's sake.

4. Even though I walk through the valley of the
shadow of death,
    I fear no evil, for You are with me;
    Your rod and Your staff, they comfort
me.

5. You prepare a table before me in the
presence of my enemies;
    You have anointed my head with oil;
    My cup overflows.

6. Surely goodness and lovingkindness will
follow me all the days of my life,
    And I will dwell in the house of the
LORD forever.

Psalm 24

1. The earth is the LORD'S, and all it contains,
   The world, and those who dwell in it.

2. For He has founded it upon the seas
   And established it upon the rivers.

3. Who may ascend into the hill of the LORD?
   And who may stand in His holy place?

4. He who has clean hands and a pure heart,
   Who has not lifted up his soul to
falsehood
   And has not sworn deceitfully.

5. He shall receive a blessing from the LORD
   And righteousness from the God of his
salvation.

6. This is the generation of those who seek Him,
   Who seek Your face — even Jacob.

7. Lift up your heads, O gates,
   And be lifted up, O ancient doors,
   That the King of glory may come in!

8. Who is the King of glory?
    The LORD strong and mighty,
    The LORD mighty in battle.

9. Lift up your heads, O gates,
    And lift them up, O ancient doors,
    That the King of glory may come in!

10. Who is this King of glory?
    The LORD of hosts,
    He is the King of glory.

Psalm 25

1. To You, O LORD, I lift up my soul.

2. O my God, in You I trust,
    Do not let me be ashamed;
    Do not let my enemies exult over me.

3. Indeed, none of those who wait for You will
be ashamed;
    Those who deal treacherously without
cause will be ashamed.

4. Make me know Your ways, O LORD;
    Teach me Your paths.

5. Lead me in Your truth and teach me,
  For You are the God of my salvation;
  For You I wait all the day.

6. Remember, O LORD, Your compassion and Your loving kindnesses,
  For they have been from of old.

7. Do not remember the sins of my youth or my transgressions;
  According to Your lovingkindness remember me,
  For Your goodness' sake, O LORD.

8. Good and upright is the LORD;
  Therefore He instructs sinners in the way.

9. He leads the humble in justice,
  And He teaches the humble His way.

10. All the paths of the LORD are lovingkindness and truth
  To those who keep His covenant and His testimonies.

11. For Your name's sake, O LORD,
  Pardon my iniquity, for it is great.

12. Who is the man who fears the LORD?
    He will instruct him in the way he
should choose.

13. His soul will abide in prosperity,
    And his descendants will inherit the
land.

14. The secret of the LORD is for those who fear
Him,
    And He will make them know His
covenant.

15. My eyes are continually toward the LORD,
    For He will pluck my feet out of the net.

16. Turn to me and be gracious to me,
    For I am lonely and afflicted.

17. The troubles of my heart are enlarged;
    Bring me out of my distresses.

18. Look upon my affliction and my trouble,
    And forgive all my sins.

19. Look upon my enemies, for they are many,
    And they hate me with violent hatred.

20. Guard my soul and deliver me;
     Do not let me be ashamed, for I take
refuge in You.

21. Let integrity and uprightness preserve me,
     For I wait for You.

22. Redeem Israel, O God,
     Out of all his troubles.

Psalm 26

1. Vindicate me, O LORD, for I have walked in
my integrity,
     And I have trusted in the LORD without
wavering.

2. Examine me, O LORD, and try me;
     Test my mind and my heart.

3. For Your lovingkindness is before my eyes,
     And I have walked in Your truth.

4. I do not sit with deceitful men,
     Nor will I go with pretenders.

5. I hate the assembly of evildoers,
     And I will not sit with the wicked.

6. I shall wash my hands in innocence,
    And I will go about Your altar, O LORD,

7. That I may proclaim with the voice of
thanksgiving
    And declare all Your wonders.

8. O LORD, I love the habitation of Your house
    And the place where Your glory dwells.

9. Do not take my soul away along with
sinners,
    Nor my life with men of bloodshed,

10. In whose hands is a wicked scheme,
    And whose right hand is full of bribes.

11. But as for me, I shall walk in my integrity;
    Redeem me, and be gracious to me.

12. My foot stands on a level place;
    In the congregations I shall bless the
LORD.

Psalm 27

1. The LORD is my light and my salvation;
    Whom shall I fear?
    The LORD is the defense of my life;
    Whom shall I dread?

2. When evildoers came upon me to devour my flesh,
    My adversaries and my enemies, they stumbled and fell.

3. Though a host encamp against me,
    My heart will not fear;
    Though war arise against me,
    In spite of this I shall be confident.

4. One thing I have asked from the LORD, that I shall seek:
    That I may dwell in the house of the LORD all the days of my life,
    To behold the beauty of the LORD
    And to meditate in His temple.

5. For in the day of trouble He will conceal me in His tabernacle;
    In the secret place of His tent He will

hide me;
        He will lift me up on a rock.

6. And now my head will be lifted up above my
enemies around me,
        And I will offer in His tent sacrifices
with shouts of joy;
        I will sing, yes, I will sing praises to the
LORD.

7. Hear, O LORD, when I cry with my voice,
        And be gracious to me and answer me.

8. When You said, "Seek My face," my heart
said to You,
        "Your face, O LORD, I shall seek."

9. Do not hide Your face from me,
        Do not turn Your servant away in anger;
        You have been my help;
        Do not abandon me nor forsake me,
        O God of my salvation!

10. For my father and my mother have forsaken
me,
        But the LORD will take me up.

11. Teach me Your way, O LORD,
>   And lead me in a level path
>   Because of my foes.

12. Do not deliver me over to the desire of my adversaries,
>   For false witnesses have risen against me,
>   And such as breathe out violence.

13. I would have despaired unless I had believed that I would see the goodness of the LORD
>   In the land of the living.

14. Wait for the LORD;
>   Be strong and let your heart take courage;
>   Yes, wait for the LORD.

Psalm 28

1. To You, O LORD, I call;
>   My rock, do not be deaf to me,
>   For if You are silent to me,
>   I will become like those who go down to the pit.

2. Hear the voice of my supplications when I cry to You for help,

When I lift up my hands toward Your holy sanctuary.

3. Do not drag me away with the wicked
And with those who work iniquity,
Who speak peace with their neighbors,
While evil is in their hearts.

4. Requite them according to their work and according to the evil of their practices;

Requite them according to the deeds of their hands;

Repay them their recompense.

5. Because they do not regard the works of the LORD

Nor the deeds of His hands,
He will tear them down and not build them up.

6. Blessed be the LORD,

Because He has heard the voice of my supplication.

7. The LORD is my strength and my shield;
My heart trusts in Him, and I am helped;

Therefore my heart exults,
And with my song I shall thank Him.

8. The LORD is their strength,
And He is a saving defense to His
anointed.

9. Save Your people and bless Your inheritance;
Be their shepherd also, and carry them
forever.

Psalm 29

1. Ascribe to the LORD, O sons of the mighty,
Ascribe to the LORD glory and strength.

2. Ascribe to the LORD the glory due to His
name;
Worship the LORD in holy array.

3. The voice of the LORD is upon the waters;
The God of glory thunders,
The LORD is over many waters.

4. The voice of the LORD is powerful,
The voice of the LORD is majestic.

5. The voice of the LORD breaks the cedars;
      Yes, the LORD breaks in pieces the
cedars of Lebanon.

6. He makes Lebanon skip like a calf,
      And Sirion like a young wild ox.

7. The voice of the LORD hews out flames of
fire.

8. The voice of the LORD shakes the
wilderness;
      The LORD shakes the wilderness of
Kadesh.

9. The voice of the LORD makes the deer to
calve
      And strips the forests bare;
      And in His temple everything says,
"Glory!"

10. The LORD sat as King at the flood;
      Yes, the LORD sits as King forever.

11. The LORD will give strength to His people;
      The LORD will bless His people with
peace.

Psalm 30

1. I will extol You, O LORD, for You have lifted me up,
   And have not let my enemies rejoice over me.

2. O LORD my God,
   I cried to You for help, and You healed me.

3. O LORD, You have brought up my soul from Sheol;
   You have kept me alive, that I would not go down to the pit.

4. Sing praise to the LORD, you His godly ones,
   And give thanks to His holy name.

5. For His anger is but for a moment,
   His favor is for a lifetime;
   Weeping may last for the night,
   But a shout of joy comes in the morning.

6. Now as for me, I said in my prosperity,
   "I will never be moved."

7. O LORD, by Your favor You have made my mountain to stand strong;

> You hid Your face, I was dismayed.

8. To You, O LORD, I called,

> And to the Lord I made supplication:

9. "What profit is there in my blood, if I go down to the pit?

> Will the dust praise You? Will it declare Your faithfulness?

10. "Hear, O LORD, and be gracious to me;

> O LORD, be my helper."

11. You have turned for me my mourning into dancing;

> You have loosed my sackcloth and girded me with gladness,

12. That my soul may sing praise to You and not be silent.

> O LORD my God, I will give thanks to You forever.

Psalm 31

1. In You, O LORD, I have taken refuge;
    Let me never be ashamed;
    In Your righteousness deliver me.

2. Incline Your ear to me, rescue me quickly;
    Be to me a rock of strength,
    A stronghold to save me.

3. For You are my rock and my fortress;
    For Your name's sake You will lead me
and guide me.

4. You will pull me out of the net which they
have secretly laid for me,
    For You are my strength.

5. Into Your hand I commit my spirit;
    You have ransomed me, O LORD, God
of truth.

6. I hate those who regard vain idols,
    But I trust in the LORD.

7. I will rejoice and be glad in Your
lovingkindness,
    Because You have seen my affliction;

You have known the troubles of my soul,

8. And You have not given me over into the hand of the enemy;
    You have set my feet in a large place.

9. Be gracious to me, O LORD, for I am in distress;
    My eye is wasted away from grief, my soul and my body also.

10. For my life is spent with sorrow
    And my years with sighing;
    My strength has failed because of my iniquity,
    And my body has wasted away.

11. Because of all my adversaries, I have become a reproach,
    Especially to my neighbors,
    And an object of dread to my acquaintances;
    Those who see me in the street flee from me.

12. I am forgotten as a dead man, out of mind;
    I am like a broken vessel.

13. For I have heard the slander of many,
        Terror is on every side;
        While they took counsel together against
me,
        They schemed to take away my life.

14. But as for me, I trust in You, O LORD,
        I say, "You are my God."

15. My times are in Your hand;
        Deliver me from the hand of my enemies
and from those who persecute me.

16. Make Your face to shine upon Your servant;
        Save me in Your lovingkindness.

17. Let me not be put to shame, O LORD, for I
call upon You;
        Let the wicked be put to shame, let them
be silent in Sheol.

18. Let the lying lips be mute,
        Which speak arrogantly against the
righteous
        With pride and contempt.

19. How great is Your goodness,
        Which You have stored up for those

who fear You,

Which You have wrought for those who take refuge in You,

Before the sons of men!

20. You hide them in the secret place of Your presence from the conspiracies of man;

You keep them secretly in a shelter from the strife of tongues.

21. Blessed be the LORD,

For He has made marvelous His lovingkindness to me in a besieged city.

22. As for me, I said in my alarm,

"I am cut off from before Your eyes";

Nevertheless You heard the voice of my supplications

When I cried to You.

23. O love the LORD, all you His godly ones!

The LORD preserves the faithful

And fully recompenses the proud doer.

24. Be strong and let your heart take courage,

All you who hope in the LORD.

Psalm 32

1. How blessed is he whose transgression is
forgiven,
> Whose sin is covered!

2. How blessed is the man to whom the LORD
does not impute iniquity,
> And in whose spirit there is no deceit!

3. When I kept silent about my sin, my body
wasted away
> Through my groaning all day long.

4. For day and night Your hand was heavy
upon me;
> My vitality was drained away as with
the fever heat of summer.

5. I acknowledged my sin to You,
> And my iniquity I did not hide;
> I said, "I will confess my transgressions
to the LORD";
> And You forgave the guilt of my sin.

6. Therefore, let everyone who is godly pray to
You in a time when You may be found;

Surely in a flood of great waters they will not reach him.

7. You are my hiding place; You preserve me from trouble;
   You surround me with songs of deliverance.

8. I will instruct you and teach you in the way which you should go;
   I will counsel you with My eye upon you.

9. Do not be as the horse or as the mule which have no understanding,
   Whose trappings include bit and bridle to hold them in check,
   Otherwise they will not come near to you.

10. Many are the sorrows of the wicked,
    But he who trusts in the LORD, lovingkindness shall surround him.

11. Be glad in the LORD and rejoice, you righteous ones;
    And shout for joy, all you who are upright in heart.

Psalm 33

1. Sing for joy in the LORD, O you righteous ones;
      Praise is becoming to the upright.

2. Give thanks to the LORD with the lyre;
      Sing praises to Him with a harp of ten strings.

3. Sing to Him a new song;
      Play skillfully with a shout of joy.

4. For the word of the LORD is upright,
      And all His work is done in faithfulness.

5. He loves righteousness and justice;
      The earth is full of the lovingkindness of the LORD.

6. By the word of the LORD the heavens were made,
      And by the breath of His mouth all their host.

7. He gathers the waters of the sea together as a heap;
      He lays up the deeps in storehouses.

8. Let all the earth fear the LORD;
    Let all the inhabitants of the world stand
in awe of Him.

9. For He spoke, and it was done;
    He commanded, and it stood fast.

10. The LORD nullifies the counsel of the
nations;
    He frustrates the plans of the peoples.

11. The counsel of the LORD stands forever,
    The plans of His heart from generation
to generation.

12. Blessed is the nation whose God is the
LORD,
    The people whom He has chosen for His
own inheritance.

13. The LORD looks from heaven;
    He sees all the sons of men;

14. From His dwelling place He looks out
    On all the inhabitants of the earth,

15. He who fashions the hearts of them all,
    He who understands all their works.

16. The king is not saved by a mighty army;
     A warrior is not delivered by great
strength.

17. A horse is a false hope for victory;
     Nor does it deliver anyone by its great
strength.

18. Behold, the eye of the LORD is on those
who fear Him,
     On those who hope for His
lovingkindness,

19. To deliver their soul from death
     And to keep them alive in famine.

20. Our soul waits for the LORD;
     He is our help and our shield.

21. For our heart rejoices in Him,
     Because we trust in His holy name.

22. Let Your lovingkindness, O LORD, be upon
us,
     According as we have hoped in You.

Psalm 34

1. I will bless the LORD at all times;
    His praise shall continually be in my mouth.

2. My soul will make its boast in the LORD;
    The humble will hear it and rejoice.

3. O magnify the LORD with me,
    And let us exalt His name together.

4. I sought the LORD, and He answered me,
    And delivered me from all my fears.

5. They looked to Him and were radiant,
    And their faces will never be ashamed.

6. This poor man cried, and the LORD heard him
    And saved him out of all his troubles.

7. The angel of the LORD encamps around those who fear Him,
    And rescues them.

8. O taste and see that the LORD is good;
    How blessed is the man who takes refuge in Him!

9. O fear the LORD, you His saints;
    For to those who fear Him there is no
want.

10. The young lions do lack and suffer hunger;
    But they who seek the LORD shall not
be in want of any good thing.

11. Come, you children, listen to me;
    I will teach you the fear of the LORD.

12. Who is the man who desires life
    And loves length of days that he may
see good?

13. Keep your tongue from evil
    And your lips from speaking deceit.

14. Depart from evil and do good;
    Seek peace and pursue it.

15. The eyes of the LORD are toward the
righteous
    And His ears are open to their cry.

16. The face of the LORD is against evildoers,
    To cut off the memory of them from the
earth.

17. The righteous cry, and the LORD hears
    And delivers them out of all their
troubles.

18. The LORD is near to the brokenhearted
    And saves those who are crushed in
spirit.

19. Many are the afflictions of the righteous,
    But the LORD delivers him out of them
all.

20. He keeps all his bones,
    Not one of them is broken.

21. Evil shall slay the wicked,
    And those who hate the righteous will
be condemned.

22. The LORD redeems the soul of His servants,
    And none of those who take refuge in
Him will be condemned.

Psalm 35

1. Contend, O LORD, with those who contend with me;
     Fight against those who fight against me.

2. Take hold of buckler and shield
     And rise up for my help.

3. Draw also the spear and the battle-axe to meet those who pursue me;
     Say to my soul, "I am your salvation."

4. Let those be ashamed and dishonored who seek my life;
     Let those be turned back and humiliated who devise evil against me.

5. Let them be like chaff before the wind,
     With the angel of the LORD driving them on.

6. Let their way be dark and slippery,
     With the angel of the LORD pursuing them.

7. For without cause they hid their net for me;
    Without cause they dug a pit for my
soul.

8. Let destruction come upon him unawares,
    And let the net which he hid catch
himself;
        Into that very destruction let him fall.

9. And my soul shall rejoice in the LORD;
    It shall exult in His salvation.

10. All my bones will say, "LORD, who is like
You,
    Who delivers the afflicted from him who
is too strong for him,
        And the afflicted and the needy from
him who robs him?"

11. Malicious witnesses rise up;
    They ask me of things that I do not
know.

12. They repay me evil for good,
    To the bereavement of my soul.

13. But as for me, when they were sick, my
clothing was sackcloth;

I humbled my soul with fasting,
And my prayer kept returning to my
bosom.

14. I went about as though it were my friend or
brother;
I bowed down mourning, as one who
sorrows for a mother.

15. But at my stumbling they rejoiced and
gathered themselves together;
The smiters whom I did not know
gathered together against me,
They slandered me without ceasing.

16. Like godless jesters at a feast,
They gnashed at me with their teeth.

17. Lord, how long will You look on?
Rescue my soul from their ravages,
My only life from the lions.

18. I will give You thanks in the great
congregation;
I will praise You among a mighty
throng.

19. Do not let those who are wrongfully my enemies rejoice over me;
Nor let those who hate me without cause wink maliciously.

20. For they do not speak peace,
But they devise deceitful words against those who are quiet in the land.

21. They opened their mouth wide against me;
They said, "Aha, aha, our eyes have seen it!"

22. You have seen it, O LORD, do not keep silent;
O Lord, do not be far from me.

23. Stir up Yourself, and awake to my right
And to my cause, my God and my Lord.

24. Judge me, O LORD my God, according to Your righteousness,
And do not let them rejoice over me.

25. Do not let them say in their heart, "Aha, our desire!"
Do not let them say, "We have swallowed him up!"

26. Let those be ashamed and humiliated altogether who rejoice at my distress;
        Let those be clothed with shame and dishonor who magnify themselves over me.

27. Let them shout for joy and rejoice, who favor my vindication;
        And let them say continually, "The LORD be magnified,
        Who delights in the prosperity of His servant."

28. And my tongue shall declare Your righteousness
        And Your praise all day long.

Psalm 36

1. Transgression speaks to the ungodly within his heart;
        There is no fear of God before his eyes.

2. For it flatters him in his own eyes
        Concerning the discovery of his iniquity and the hatred of it.

3. The words of his mouth are wickedness and deceit;

He has ceased to be wise and to do good.

4. He plans wickedness upon his bed;

He sets himself on a path that is not good;

He does not despise evil.

5. Your lovingkindness, O LORD, extends to the heavens,

Your faithfulness reaches to the skies.

6. Your righteousness is like the mountains of God;

Your judgments are like a great deep.
O LORD, You preserve man and beast.

7. How precious is Your lovingkindness, O God!

And the children of men take refuge in the shadow of Your wings.

8. They drink their fill of the abundance of Your house;

And You give them to drink of the river of Your delights.

9. For with You is the fountain of life;
     In Your light we see light.

10. O continue Your lovingkindness to those
who know You,
     And Your righteousness to the upright
in heart.

11. Let not the foot of pride come upon me,
     And let not the hand of the wicked drive
me away.

12. There the doers of iniquity have fallen;
     They have been thrust down and cannot
rise.

Psalm 37

1. Do not fret because of evildoers,
     Be not envious toward wrongdoers.

2. For they will wither quickly like the grass
     And fade like the green herb.

3. Trust in the LORD and do good;
     Dwell in the land and cultivate
faithfulness.

4. Delight yourself in the LORD;
>And He will give you the desires of your heart.

5. Commit your way to the LORD,
>Trust also in Him, and He will do it.

6. He will bring forth your righteousness as the light
>And your judgment as the noonday.

7. Rest in the LORD and wait patiently for Him;
>Do not fret because of him who prospers in his way,
>Because of the man who carries out wicked schemes.

8. Cease from anger and forsake wrath;
>Do not fret; it leads only to evildoing.

9. For evildoers will be cut off,
>But those who wait for the LORD, they will inherit the land.

10. Yet a little while and the wicked man will be no more;
>And you will look carefully for his place and he will not be there.

11. But the humble will inherit the land
    And will delight themselves in abundant
prosperity.

12. The wicked plots against the righteous
    And gnashes at him with his teeth.

13. The Lord laughs at him,
    For He sees his day is coming.

14. The wicked have drawn the sword and bent
their bow
    To cast down the afflicted and the
needy,
    To slay those who are upright in
conduct.

15. Their sword will enter their own heart,
    And their bows will be broken.

16. Better is the little of the righteous
    Than the abundance of many wicked.

17. For the arms of the wicked will be broken,
    But the LORD sustains the righteous.

18. The LORD knows the days of the blameless,
    And their inheritance will be forever.

19. They will not be ashamed in the time of evil,
　　And in the days of famine they will have abundance.

20. But the wicked will perish;
　　And the enemies of the LORD will be like the glory of the pastures,
　　They vanish—like smoke they vanish away.

21. The wicked borrows and does not pay back,
　　But the righteous is gracious and gives.

22. For those blessed by Him will inherit the land,
　　But those cursed by Him will be cut off.

23. The steps of a man are established by the LORD,
　　And He delights in his way.

24. When he falls, he will not be hurled headlong,
　　Because the LORD is the One who holds his hand.

25. I have been young and now I am old,
　　Yet I have not seen the righteous

forsaken
Or his descendants begging bread.

26. All day long he is gracious and lends,
And his descendants are a blessing.

27. Depart from evil and do good,
So you will abide forever.

28. For the LORD loves justice
And does not forsake His godly ones;
They are preserved forever,
But the descendants of the wicked will
be cut off.

29. The righteous will inherit the land
And dwell in it forever.

30. The mouth of the righteous utters wisdom,
And his tongue speaks justice.

31. The law of his God is in his heart;
His steps do not slip.

32. The wicked spies on the righteous
And seeks to kill him.

33. The LORD will not leave him in his hand
     Or let him be condemned when he is
judged.

34. Wait for the LORD and keep His way,
     And He will exalt you to inherit the
land;
     When the wicked are cut off, you will
see it.

35. I have seen a wicked, violent man
     Spreading himself like a luxuriant tree in
its native soil.

36. Then he passed away, and lo, he was no
more;
     I sought for him, but he could not be
found.

37. Mark the blameless man, and behold the
upright;
     For the man of peace will have a
posterity.

38. But transgressors will be altogether
destroyed;
     The posterity of the wicked will be cut
off.

39. But the salvation of the righteous is from the LORD;

> He is their strength in time of trouble.

40. The LORD helps them and delivers them;

> He delivers them from the wicked and

saves them,

> Because they take refuge in Him.

Psalm 38

1. O LORD, rebuke me not in Your wrath,

> And chasten me not in Your burning

anger.

2. For Your arrows have sunk deep into me,

> And Your hand has pressed down on

me.

3. There is no soundness in my flesh because of Your indignation;

> There is no health in my bones because

of my sin.

4. For my iniquities are gone over my head;

> As a heavy burden they weigh too much

for me.

5. My wounds grow foul and fester
     Because of my folly.

6. I am bent over and greatly bowed down;
     I go mourning all day long.

7. For my loins are filled with burning,
     And there is no soundness in my flesh.

8. I am benumbed and badly crushed;
     I groan because of the agitation of my
heart.

9. Lord, all my desire is before You;
     And my sighing is not hidden from You.

10. My heart throbs, my strength fails me;
     And the light of my eyes, even that has
gone from me.

11. My loved ones and my friends stand aloof
from my plague;
     And my kinsmen stand afar off.

12. Those who seek my life lay snares for me;
     And those who seek to injure me have
threatened destruction,
     And they devise treachery all day long.

13. But I, like a deaf man, do not hear;
      And I am like a mute man who does not
open his mouth.

14. Yes, I am like a man who does not hear,
      And in whose mouth are no arguments.

15. For I hope in You, O LORD;
      You will answer, O Lord my God.

16. For I said, "May they not rejoice over me,
      Who, when my foot slips, would
magnify themselves against me."

17. For I am ready to fall,
      And my sorrow is continually before
me.

18. For I confess my iniquity;
      I am full of anxiety because of my sin.

19. But my enemies are vigorous and strong,
      And many are those who hate me
wrongfully.

20. And those who repay evil for good,
      They oppose me, because I follow what
is good.

21. Do not forsake me, O LORD;
     O my God, do not be far from me!

22. Make haste to help me,
     O Lord, my salvation!

Psalm 39

1. I said, "I will guard my ways
     That I may not sin with my tongue;
     I will guard my mouth as with a muzzle
     While the wicked are in my presence."

2. I was mute and silent,
     I refrained even from good,
     And my sorrow grew worse.

3. My heart was hot within me,
     While I was musing the fire burned;
     Then I spoke with my tongue:

4. "LORD, make me to know my end
     And what is the extent of my days;
     Let me know how transient I am.

5. "Behold, You have made my days as
handbreadths,

And my lifetime as nothing in Your sight;
　　Surely every man at his best is a mere breath.

6. "Surely every man walks about as a phantom;
　　Surely they make an uproar for nothing;
　　He amasses riches and does not know who will gather them.

7. "And now, Lord, for what do I wait?
　　My hope is in You.

8. "Deliver me from all my transgressions;
　　Make me not the reproach of the foolish.

9. "I have become mute, I do not open my mouth,
　　Because it is You who have done it.

10. "Remove Your plague from me;
　　Because of the opposition of Your hand I am perishing.

11. "With reproofs You chasten a man for iniquity;
　　You consume as a moth what is precious

to him;
>Surely every man is a mere breath.

12. "Hear my prayer, O LORD, and give ear to my cry;
>Do not be silent at my tears;
>For I am a stranger with You,
>A sojourner like all my fathers.

13. "Turn Your gaze away from me, that I may smile *again*
>Before I depart and am no more."

Psalm 40

1. I waited patiently for the LORD;
>And He inclined to me and heard my
cry.

2. He brought me up out of the pit of destruction, out of the miry clay,
>And He set my feet upon a rock making
my footsteps firm.

3. He put a new song in my mouth, a song of praise to our God;

Many will see and fear
And will trust in the LORD.

4. How blessed is the man who has made the LORD his trust,
And has not turned to the proud, nor to those who lapse into falsehood.

5. Many, O LORD my God, are the wonders which You have done,
And Your thoughts toward us;
There is none to compare with You.
If I would declare and speak of them,
They would be too numerous to count.

6. Sacrifice and meal offering You have not desired;
My ears You have opened;
Burnt offering and sin offering You have not required.

7. Then I said, "Behold, I come;
In the scroll of the book it is written of me.

8. I delight to do Your will, O my God;
Your Law is within my heart."

9. I have proclaimed glad tidings of
righteousness in the great congregation;
>Behold, I will not restrain my lips,
>O LORD, You know.

10. I have not hidden Your righteousness
within my heart;
>I have spoken of Your faithfulness and
Your salvation;
>I have not concealed Your
lovingkindness and Your truth from the great
congregation.

11. You, O LORD, will not withhold Your
compassion from me;
>Your lovingkindness and Your truth will
continually preserve me.

12. For evils beyond number have surrounded
me;
>My iniquities have overtaken me, so that
I am not able to see;
>They are more numerous than the hairs
of my head,
>And my heart has failed me.

13. Be pleased, O LORD, to deliver me;
>Make haste, O LORD, to help me.

14. Let those be ashamed and humiliated together
>Who seek my life to destroy it;
>Let those be turned back and dishonored
>Who delight in my hurt.

15. Let those be appalled because of their shame
>Who say to me, "Aha, aha!"

16. Let all who seek You rejoice and be glad in You;
>Let those who love Your salvation say continually,
>"The LORD be magnified!"

17. Since I am afflicted and needy,
>Let the Lord be mindful of me.
>You are my help and my deliverer;
>Do not delay, O my God.

Psalm 41

1. How blessed is he who considers the helpless;
> The LORD will deliver him in a day of trouble.

2. The LORD will protect him and keep him alive,
> And he shall be called blessed upon the earth;
> And do not give him over to the desire of his enemies.

3. The LORD will sustain him upon his sickbed;
> In his illness, You restore him to health.

4. As for me, I said, "O LORD, be gracious to me;
> Heal my soul, for I have sinned against You."

5. My enemies speak evil against me,
> "When will he die, and his name perish?"

6. And when he comes to see me, he speaks falsehood;

His heart gathers wickedness to itself;
When he goes outside, he tells it.

7. All who hate me whisper together against
me;
Against me they devise my hurt, saying,

8. "A wicked thing is poured out upon him,
That when he lies down, he will not rise
up again."

9. Even my close friend in whom I trusted,
Who ate my bread,
Has lifted up his heel against me.

10. But You, O LORD, be gracious to me and
raise me up,
That I may repay them.

11. By this I know that You are pleased with
me,
Because my enemy does not shout in
triumph over me.

12. As for me, You uphold me in my integrity,
And You set me in Your presence
forever.

13. Blessed be the LORD, the God of Israel,
      From everlasting to everlasting.
      Amen and Amen.

Psalm 42

1. As the deer pants for the water brooks,
      So my soul pants for You, O God.

2. My soul thirsts for God, for the living God;
      When shall I come and appear before
God?

3. My tears have been my food day and night,
      While they say to me all day long,
"Where is your God?"

4. These things I remember and I pour out my
soul within me.
      For I used to go along with the throng
and lead them in procession to the house of
God,
      With the voice of joy and thanksgiving, a
multitude keeping festival.

5. Why are you in despair, O my soul?
      And why have you become disturbed

within me?

Hope in God, for I shall again praise Him

For the help of His presence.

6. O my God, my soul is in despair within me;

Therefore I remember You from the land of the Jordan

And the peaks of Hermon, from Mount Mizar.

7. Deep calls to deep at the sound of Your waterfalls;

All Your breakers and Your waves have rolled over me.

8. The LORD will command His lovingkindness in the daytime;

And His song will be with me in the night,

A prayer to the God of my life.

9. I will say to God my rock, "Why have You forgotten me?

Why do I go mourning because of the oppression of the enemy?"

10. As a shattering of my bones, my adversaries revile me,
    While they say to me all day long, "Where is your God?"

11. Why are you in despair, O my soul?
    And why have you become disturbed within me?
    Hope in God, for I shall yet praise Him,
    The help of my countenance and my God.

Psalm 43

1. Vindicate me, O God, and plead my case against an ungodly nation;
    O deliver me from the deceitful and unjust man!

2. For You are the God of my strength; why have You rejected me?
    Why do I go mourning because of the oppression of the enemy?

3. O send out Your light and Your truth, let them lead me;

Let them bring me to Your holy hill
And to Your dwelling places.

4. Then I will go to the altar of God,
    To God my exceeding joy;
    And upon the lyre I shall praise You, O
God, my God.

5. Why are you in despair, O my soul?
    And why are you disturbed within me?
    Hope in God, for I shall again praise
Him,
    The help of my countenance and my
God.

Psalm 44

1. O God, we have heard with our ears,
    Our fathers have told us
    The work that You did in their days,
    In the days of old.

2. You with Your own hand drove out the
nations;
    Then You planted them;
    You afflicted the peoples,
    Then You spread them abroad.

3. For by their own sword they did not possess the land,
>And their own arm did not save them,
>But Your right hand and Your arm and the light of Your presence,
>For You favored them.

4. You are my King, O God;
>Command victories for Jacob.

5. Through You we will push back our adversaries;
>Through Your name we will trample down those who rise up against us.

6. For I will not trust in my bow,
>Nor will my sword save me.

7. But You have saved us from our adversaries,
>And You have put to shame those who hate us.

8. In God we have boasted all day long,
>And we will give thanks to Your name forever.

9. Yet You have rejected us and brought us to dishonor,

   And do not go out with our armies.

10. You cause us to turn back from the adversary;

   And those who hate us have taken spoil for themselves.

11. You give us as sheep to be eaten

   And have scattered us among the nations.

12. You sell Your people cheaply,

   And have not profited by their sale.

13. You make us a reproach to our neighbors,

   A scoffing and a derision to those around us.

14. You make us a byword among the nations,

   A laughingstock among the peoples.

15. All day long my dishonor is before me

   And my humiliation has overwhelmed me,

16. Because of the voice of him who reproaches and reviles,

Because of the presence of the enemy
and the avenger.

17. All this has come upon us, but we have not
forgotten You,
And we have not dealt falsely with Your
covenant.

18. Our heart has not turned back,
And our steps have not deviated from
Your way,

19. Yet You have crushed us in a place of
jackals
And covered us with the shadow of
death.

20. If we had forgotten the name of our God
Or extended our hands to a strange god,

21. Would not God find this out?
For He knows the secrets of the heart.

22. But for Your sake we are killed all day long;
We are considered as sheep to be
slaughtered.

23. Arouse Yourself, why do You sleep, O Lord?
> Awake, do not reject us forever.

24. Why do You hide Your face
> And forget our affliction and our oppression?

25. For our soul has sunk down into the dust;
> Our body cleaves to the earth.

26. Rise up, be our help,
> And redeem us for the sake of Your lovingkindness.

Psalm 45

1. My heart overflows with a good theme;
> I address my verses to the King;
> My tongue is the pen of a ready writer.

2. You are fairer than the sons of men;
> Grace is poured upon Your lips;
> Therefore God has blessed You forever.

3. Gird Your sword on Your thigh, O Mighty One,

> In Your splendor and Your majesty!

4. And in Your majesty ride on victoriously,

> For the cause of truth and meekness and righteousness;

> Let Your right hand teach You awesome things.

5. Your arrows are sharp;

> The peoples fall under You;

> Your arrows are in the heart of the King's enemies.

6. Your throne, O God, is forever and ever;

> A scepter of uprightness is the scepter of Your kingdom.

7. You have loved righteousness and hated wickedness;

> Therefore God, Your God, has anointed You

> With the oil of joy above Your fellows.

8. All Your garments are fragrant with myrrh and aloes and cassia;

Out of ivory palaces stringed instruments have made You glad.

9. Kings' daughters are among Your noble ladies;
     At Your right hand stands the queen in gold from Ophir.

10. Listen, O daughter, give attention and incline your ear:
     Forget your people and your father's house;

11. Then the King will desire your beauty.
     Because He is your Lord, bow down to Him.

12. The daughter of Tyre will come with a gift;
     The rich among the people will seek your favor.

13. The King's daughter is all glorious within;
     Her clothing is interwoven with gold.

14. She will be led to the King in embroidered work;
     The virgins, her companions who follow

her,
> Will be brought to You.

15. They will be led forth with gladness and rejoicing;
> They will enter into the King's palace.

16. In place of your fathers will be your sons;
> You shall make them princes in all the earth.

17. I will cause Your name to be remembered in all generations;
> Therefore the peoples will give You thanks forever and ever.

Psalm 46

1. God is our refuge and strength,
> A very present help in trouble.

2. Therefore we will not fear, though the earth should change
> And though the mountains slip into the heart of the sea;

3. Though its waters roar and foam,
    Though the mountains quake at its swelling pride.

4. There is a river whose streams make glad the city of God,
    The holy dwelling places of the Most High.

5. God is in the midst of her, she will not be moved;
    God will help her when morning dawns.

6. The nations made an uproar, the kingdoms tottered;
    He raised His voice, the earth melted.

7. The LORD of hosts is with us;
    The God of Jacob is our stronghold.

8. Come, behold the works of the LORD,
    Who has wrought desolations in the earth.

9. He makes wars to cease to the end of the earth;
    He breaks the bow and cuts the spear in

two;
>He burns the chariots with fire.

10. "Cease striving and know that I am God;
>I will be exalted among the nations, I
will be exalted in the earth."

11. The LORD of hosts is with us;
>The God of Jacob is our stronghold.

Psalm 47

1. O clap your hands, all peoples;
>Shout to God with the voice of joy.

2. For the LORD Most High is to be feared,
>A great King over all the earth.

3. He subdues peoples under us
>And nations under our feet.

4. He chooses our inheritance for us,
>The glory of Jacob whom He loves.

5. God has ascended with a shout,
>The LORD, with the sound of a trumpet.

6. Sing praises to God, sing praises;
     Sing praises to our King, sing praises.

7. For God is the King of all the earth;
     Sing praises with a skillful psalm.

8. God reigns over the nations,
     God sits on His holy throne.

9. The princes of the people have assembled
themselves *as* the people of the God of
Abraham,
     For the shields of the earth belong to
God;
     He is highly exalted.

Psalm 48

1. Great is the LORD, and greatly to be praised,
     In the city of our God, His holy
mountain.

2. Beautiful in elevation, the joy of the whole
earth,
     Is Mount Zion in the far north,
     The city of the great King.

3. God, in her palaces,
> Has made Himself known as a
stronghold.

4. For, lo, the kings assembled themselves,
> They passed by together.

5. They saw it, then they were amazed;
> They were terrified, they fled in alarm.

6. Panic seized them there,
> Anguish, as of a woman in childbirth.

7. With the east wind
> You break the ships of Tarshish.

8. As we have heard, so have we seen
> In the city of the LORD of hosts, in the
city of our God;
> God will establish her forever.

9. We have thought on Your lovingkindness, O
God,
> In the midst of Your temple.

10. As is Your name, O God,
> So is Your praise to the ends of the earth;
> Your right hand is full of righteousness.

11. Let Mount Zion be glad,
    Let the daughters of Judah rejoice
    Because of Your judgments.

12. Walk about Zion and go around her;
    Count her towers;

13. Consider her ramparts;
    Go through her palaces,
    That you may tell it to the next
generation.

14. For such is God,
    Our God forever and ever;
    He will guide us until death.

Psalm 49

1. Hear this, all peoples;
    Give ear, all inhabitants of the world,

2. Both low and high,
    Rich and poor together.

3. My mouth will speak wisdom,
    And the meditation of my heart will be
understanding.

4. I will incline my ear to a proverb;
   I will express my riddle on the harp.

5. Why should I fear in days of adversity,
   When the iniquity of my foes surrounds
me,

6. Even those who trust in their wealth
   And boast in the abundance of their
riches?

7. No man can by any means redeem his
brother
   Or give to God a ransom for him—

8. For the redemption of his soul is costly,
   And he should cease trying forever—

9. That he should live on eternally,
   That he should not undergo decay.

10. For he sees that even wise men die;
    The stupid and the senseless alike perish
    And leave their wealth to others.

11. Their inner thought is that their houses are
forever
    And their dwelling places to all
generations;

They have called their lands after their own names.

12. But man in his pomp will not endure;
   He is like the beasts that perish.

13. This is the way of those who are foolish,
   And of those after them who approve their words.

14. As sheep they are appointed for Sheol;
   Death shall be their shepherd;
   And the upright shall rule over them in the morning,
   And their form shall be for Sheol to consume
   So that they have no habitation.

15. But God will redeem my soul from the power of Sheol,
   For He will receive me.

16. Do not be afraid when a man becomes rich,
   When the glory of his house is increased;

17. For when he dies he will carry nothing away;
   His glory will not descend after him.

18. Though while he lives he congratulates himself—

And though men praise you when you do well for yourself—

19. He shall go to the generation of his fathers;
They will never see the light.

20. Man in his pomp, yet without understanding,
Is like the beasts that perish.

Psalm 50

1. The Mighty One, God, the LORD, has spoken,
And summoned the earth from the rising of the sun to its setting.

2. Out of Zion, the perfection of beauty,
God has shone forth.

3. May our God come and not keep silence;
Fire devours before Him,
And it is very tempestuous around Him.

4. He summons the heavens above,
And the earth, to judge His people:

5. "Gather My godly ones to Me,
Those who have made a covenant with
Me by sacrifice."

6. And the heavens declare His righteousness,
For God Himself is judge.

7. "Hear, O My people, and I will speak;
O Israel, I will testify against you;
I am God, your God.

8. "I do not reprove you for your sacrifices,
And your burnt offerings are continually
before Me.

9. "I shall take no young bull out of your house
Nor male goats out of your folds.

10. "For every beast of the forest is Mine,
The cattle on a thousand hills.

11. "I know every bird of the mountains,
And everything that moves in the field is
Mine.

12. "If I were hungry I would not tell you,
     For the world is Mine, and all it contains.

13. "Shall I eat the flesh of bulls
     Or drink the blood of male goats?

14. "Offer to God a sacrifice of thanksgiving
     And pay your vows to the Most High;

15. Call upon Me in the day of trouble;
     I shall rescue you, and you will honor
Me."

16. But to the wicked God says,
     "What right have you to tell of My statutes
     And to take My covenant in your mouth?

17. "For you hate discipline,
     And you cast My words behind you.

18. "When you see a thief, you are pleased with him,
     And you associate with adulterers.

19. "You let your mouth loose in evil
     And your tongue frames deceit.

20. "You sit and speak against your brother;
      You slander your own mother's son.

21. "These things you have done and I kept silence;
      You thought that I was just like you;
      I will reprove you and state the case in order before your eyes.

22. "Now consider this, you who forget God,
      Or I will tear you in pieces, and there will be none to deliver.

23. "He who offers a sacrifice of thanksgiving honors Me;
      And to him who orders his way aright I shall show the salvation of God."

Psalm 51

1. Be gracious to me, O God, according to Your lovingkindness;
      According to the greatness of Your compassion blot out my transgressions.

2. Wash me thoroughly from my iniquity
      And cleanse me from my sin.

3. For I know my transgressions,
    And my sin is ever before me.

4. Against You, You only, I have sinned
    And done what is evil in Your sight,
    So that You are justified when You speak
    And blameless when You judge.

5. Behold, I was brought forth in iniquity,
    And in sin my mother conceived me.

6. Behold, You desire truth in the innermost being,
    And in the hidden part You will make me know wisdom.

7. Purify me with hyssop, and I shall be clean;
    Wash me, and I shall be whiter than snow.

8. Make me to hear joy and gladness,
    Let the bones which You have broken rejoice.

9. Hide Your face from my sins
    And blot out all my iniquities.

10. Create in me a clean heart, O God,
    And renew a steadfast spirit within me.

11. Do not cast me away from Your presence
    And do not take Your Holy Spirit from
me.

12. Restore to me the joy of Your salvation
    And sustain me with a willing spirit.

13. Then I will teach transgressors Your ways,
    And sinners will be converted to You.

14. Deliver me from blood guiltiness, O God,
the God of my salvation;
    Then my tongue will joyfully sing of
Your righteousness.

15. O Lord, open my lips,
    That my mouth may declare Your
praise.

16. For You do not delight in sacrifice,
otherwise I would give it;
    You are not pleased with burnt offering.

17. The sacrifices of God are a broken spirit;
    A broken and a contrite heart, O God,
You will not despise.

18. By Your favor do good to Zion;
    Build the walls of Jerusalem.

19. Then You will delight in righteous
sacrifices,
    In burnt offering and whole burnt
offering;
    Then young bulls will be offered on
Your altar.

Psalm 52

1. Why do you boast in evil, O mighty man?
    The lovingkindness of God endures all
day long.

2. Your tongue devises destruction,
    Like a sharp razor, O worker of deceit.

3. You love evil more than good,
    Falsehood more than speaking what is
right.

4. You love all words that devour,
    O deceitful tongue.

5. But God will break you down forever;
   He will snatch you up and tear you
away from your tent,
   And uproot you from the land of the
living.

6. The righteous will see and fear,
   And will laugh at him, saying,

7. "Behold, the man who would not make God
his refuge,
   But trusted in the abundance of his
riches
   And was strong in his evil desire."

8. But as for me, I am like a green olive tree in
the house of God;
   I trust in the lovingkindness of God
forever and ever.

9. I will give You thanks forever, because You
have done it,
   And I will wait on Your name, for it is
good, in the presence of Your godly ones.

Psalm 53

1. The fool has said in his heart, "There is no God,"
    They are corrupt, and have committed abominable injustice;
    There is no one who does good.

2. God has looked down from heaven upon the sons of men
    To see if there is anyone who understands,
    Who seeks after God.

3. Every one of them has turned aside; together they have become corrupt;
    There is no one who does good, not even one.

4. Have the workers of wickedness no knowledge,
    Who eat up My people as though they ate bread
    And have not called upon God?

5. There they were in great fear where no fear had been;
    For God scattered the bones of him who

encamped against you;
　　You put them to shame, because God had rejected them.

6. Oh, that the salvation of Israel would come out of Zion!
　　When God restores His captive people,
　　Let Jacob rejoice, let Israel be glad.

Psalm 54

1. Save me, O God, by Your name,
　　And vindicate me by Your power.

2. Hear my prayer, O God;
　　Give ear to the words of my mouth.

3. For strangers have risen against me
　　And violent men have sought my life;
　　They have not set God before them.

4. Behold, God is my helper;
　　The Lord is the sustainer of my soul.

5. He will recompense the evil to my foes;
　　Destroy them in Your faithfulness.

6. Willingly I will sacrifice to You;
    I will give thanks to Your name, O
LORD, for it is good.

7. For He has delivered me from all trouble,
    And my eye has looked with satisfaction
upon my enemies.

Psalm 55

1. Give ear to my prayer, O God;
    And do not hide Yourself from my
supplication.

2. Give heed to me and answer me;
    I am restless in my complaint and am
surely distracted,

3. Because of the voice of the enemy,
    Because of the pressure of the wicked;
    For they bring down trouble upon me
    And in anger they bear a grudge against
me.

4. My heart is in anguish within me,
    And the terrors of death have fallen
upon me.

5. Fear and trembling come upon me,
   And horror has overwhelmed me.

6. I said, "Oh, that I had wings like a dove!
   I would fly away and be at rest.

7. "Behold, I would wander far away,
   I would lodge in the wilderness.

8. "I would hasten to my place of refuge
   From the stormy wind and tempest."

9. Confuse, O Lord, divide their tongues,
   For I have seen violence and strife in the city.

10. Day and night they go around her upon her walls,
    And iniquity and mischief are in her midst.

11. Destruction is in her midst;
    Oppression and deceit do not depart from her streets.

12. For it is not an enemy who reproaches me,
    Then I could bear it;
    Nor is it one who hates me who has

exalted himself against me,
　　Then I could hide myself from him.

13. But it is you, a man my equal,
　　My companion and my familiar friend;

14. We who had sweet fellowship together
　　Walked in the house of God in the
throng.

15. Let death come deceitfully upon them;
　　Let them go down alive to Sheol,
　　For evil is in their dwelling, in their
midst.

16. As for me, I shall call upon God,
　　And the LORD will save me.

17. Evening and morning and at noon, I will
complain and murmur,
　　And He will hear my voice.

18. He will redeem my soul in peace from the
battle which is against me,
　　For they are many who strive with me.

19. God will hear and answer them —
　　Even the one who sits enthroned from of
old —

With whom there is no change,
And who do not fear God.

20. He has put forth his hands against those who were at peace with him;
He has violated his covenant.

21. His speech was smoother than butter,
But his heart was war;
His words were softer than oil,
Yet they were drawn swords.

22. Cast your burden upon the LORD and He will sustain you;
He will never allow the righteous to be shaken.

23. But You, O God, will bring them down to the pit of destruction;
Men of bloodshed and deceit will not live out half their days.
But I will trust in You.

Psalm 56

1. Be gracious to me, O God, for man has
trampled upon me;
    Fighting all day long he oppresses me.

2. My foes have trampled upon me all day
long,
    For they are many who fight proudly
against me.

3. When I am afraid,
    I will put my trust in You.

4. In God, whose word I praise,
    In God I have put my trust;
    I shall not be afraid.
    What can mere man do to me?

5. All day long they distort my words;
    All their thoughts are against me for
evil.

6. They attack, they lurk,
    They watch my steps,
    As they have waited to take my life.

7. Because of wickedness, cast them forth,
     In anger put down the peoples, O God!

8. You have taken account of my wanderings;
     Put my tears in Your bottle.
     Are they not in Your book?

9. Then my enemies will turn back in the day when I call;
     This I know, that God is for me.

10. In God, whose word I praise,
     In the LORD, whose word I praise,

11. In God I have put my trust, I shall not be afraid.
     What can man do to me?

12. Your vows are binding upon me, O God;
     I will render thank offerings to You.

13. For You have delivered my soul from death,
     Indeed my feet from stumbling,
     So that I may walk before God
     In the light of the living.

Psalm 57

1. Be gracious to me, O God, be gracious to me,
     For my soul takes refuge in You;
     And in the shadow of Your wings I will
take refuge
     Until destruction passes by.

2. I will cry to God Most High,
     To God who accomplishes all things for
me.

3. He will send from heaven and save me;
     He reproaches him who tramples upon
me.
     God will send forth His lovingkindness
and His truth.

4. My soul is among lions;
     I must lie among those who breathe
forth fire,
     Even the sons of men, whose teeth are
spears and arrows
     And their tongue a sharp sword.

5. Be exalted above the heavens, O God;
     Let Your glory be above all the earth.

6. They have prepared a net for my steps;
   My soul is bowed down;
   They dug a pit before me;
   They themselves have fallen into the
midst of it.

7. My heart is steadfast, O God, my heart is
steadfast;
   I will sing, yes, I will sing praises!

8. Awake, my glory!
   Awake, harp and lyre!
   I will awaken the dawn.

9. I will give thanks to You, O Lord, among the
peoples;
   I will sing praises to You among the
nations.

10. For Your lovingkindness is great to the
heavens
   And Your truth to the clouds.

11. Be exalted above the heavens, O God;
   Let Your glory be above all the earth.

Psalm 58

1. Do you indeed speak righteousness, O gods?
        Do you judge uprightly, O sons of men?

2. No, in heart you work unrighteousness;
        On earth you weigh out the violence of
your hands.

3. The wicked are estranged from the womb;
        These who speak lies go astray from
birth.

4. They have venom like the venom of a
serpent;
        Like a deaf cobra that stops up its ear,

5. So that it does not hear the voice of charmers,
        Or a skillful caster of spells.

6. O God, shatter their teeth in their mouth;
        Break out the fangs of the young lions, O
LORD.

7. Let them flow away like water that runs off;
        When he aims his arrows, let them be as
headless shafts.

8. Let them be as a snail which melts away as it goes along,

 Like the miscarriages of a woman which never see the sun.

9. Before your pots can feel the fire of thorns

 He will sweep them away with a whirlwind, the green and the burning alike.

10. The righteous will rejoice when he sees the vengeance;

 He will wash his feet in the blood of the wicked.

11. And men will say, "Surely there is a reward for the righteous;

 Surely there is a God who judges on earth!"

Psalm 59

1. Deliver me from my enemies, O my God;

 Set me securely on high away from those who rise up against me.

2. Deliver me from those who do iniquity

 And save me from men of bloodshed.

3. For behold, they have set an ambush for my life;

> Fierce men launch an attack against me,
> Not for my transgression nor for my sin,

O LORD,

4. For no guilt of mine, they run and set themselves against me.

> Arouse Yourself to help me, and see!

5. You, O LORD God of hosts, the God of Israel,

> Awake to punish all the nations;
> Do not be gracious to any who are

treacherous in iniquity.

6. They return at evening, they howl like a dog,

> And go around the city.

7. Behold, they belch forth with their mouth;

> Swords are in their lips,
> For, they say, "Who hears?"

8. But You, O LORD, laugh at them;

> You scoff at all the nations.

9. Because of his strength I will watch for You,

> For God is my stronghold.

10. My God in His lovingkindness will meet me;
  God will let me look triumphantly upon my foes.

11. Do not slay them, or my people will forget;
  Scatter them by Your power, and bring them down,
  O Lord, our shield.

12. On account of the sin of their mouth and the words of their lips,
  Let them even be caught in their pride,
  And on account of curses and lies which they utter.

13. Destroy them in wrath, destroy them that they may be no more;
  That men may know that God rules in Jacob
  To the ends of the earth.

14. They return at evening, they howl like a dog,
  And go around the city.

15. They wander about for food
  And growl if they are not satisfied.

16. But as for me, I shall sing of Your strength;
 Yes, I shall joyfully sing of Your
lovingkindness in the morning,
 For You have been my stronghold
 And a refuge in the day of my distress.

17. O my strength, I will sing praises to You;
 For God is my stronghold, the God who
shows me lovingkindness.

Psalm 60

1. O God, You have rejected us. You have
broken us;
 You have been angry; O, restore us.

2. You have made the land quake, You have
split it open;
 Heal its breaches, for it totters.

3. You have made Your people experience
hardship;
 You have given us wine to drink that
makes us stagger.

4. You have given a banner to those who fear
You,

That it may be displayed because of the truth.

5. That Your beloved may be delivered,
    Save with Your right hand, and answer us!

6. God has spoken in His holiness:
    "I will exult, I will portion out Shechem and measure out the valley of Succoth.

7. "Gilead is Mine, and Manasseh is Mine;
    Ephraim also is the helmet of My head;
    Judah is My scepter.

8. "Moab is My washbowl;
    Over Edom I shall throw My shoe;
    Shout loud, O Philistia, because of Me!"

9. Who will bring me into the besieged city?
    Who will lead me to Edom?

10. Have not You Yourself, O God, rejected us?
    And will You not go forth with our armies, O God?

11. O give us help against the adversary,
    For deliverance by man is in vain.

12. Through God we shall do valiantly,
	And it is He who will tread down our adversaries.

Psalm 61

1. Hear my cry, O God;
	Give heed to my prayer.

2. From the end of the earth I call to You when my heart is faint;
	Lead me to the rock that is higher than I.

3. For You have been a refuge for me,
	A tower of strength against the enemy.

4. Let me dwell in Your tent forever;
	Let me take refuge in the shelter of Your wings.

5. For You have heard my vows, O God;
	You have given me the inheritance of those who fear Your name.

6. You will prolong the king's life;
	His years will be as many generations.

7. He will abide before God forever;
    Appoint lovingkindness and truth that
they may preserve him.

8. So I will sing praise to Your name forever,
    That I may pay my vows day by day.

Psalm 62

1. My soul waits in silence for God only;
    From Him is my salvation.

2. He only is my rock and my salvation,
    My stronghold; I shall not be greatly
shaken.

3. How long will you assail a man,
    That you may murder him, all of you,
    Like a leaning wall, like a tottering
fence?

4. They have counseled only to thrust him
down from his high position;
    They delight in falsehood;
    They bless with their mouth,
    But inwardly they curse.

5. My soul, wait in silence for God only,
      For my hope is from Him.

6. He only is my rock and my salvation,
      My stronghold; I shall not be shaken.

7. On God my salvation and my glory rest;
      The rock of my strength, my refuge is in
God.

8. Trust in Him at all times, O people;
      Pour out your heart before Him;
      God is a refuge for us.

9. Men of low degree are only vanity and men
of rank are a lie;
      In the balances they go up;
      They are together lighter than breath.

10. Do not trust in oppression
      And do not vainly hope in robbery;
      If riches increase, do not set your heart
upon them.

11. Once God has spoken;
      Twice I have heard this:
      That power belongs to God;

12. And lovingkindness is Yours, O Lord,
    For You recompense a man according to
his work.

Psalm 63

1. O God, You are my God; I shall seek You
earnestly;
    My soul thirsts for You, my flesh yearns
for You,
    In a dry and weary land where there is
no water.

2. Thus I have seen You in the sanctuary,
    To see Your power and Your glory.

3. Because Your lovingkindness is better than
life,
    My lips will praise You.

4. So I will bless You as long as I live;
    I will lift up my hands in Your name.

5. My soul is satisfied as with marrow and
fatness,
    And my mouth offers praises with joyful
lips.

6. When I remember You on my bed,
     I meditate on You in the night watches,

7. For You have been my help,
     And in the shadow of Your wings I sing
for joy.

8. My soul clings to You;
     Your right hand upholds me.

9. But those who seek my life to destroy it,
     Will go into the depths of the earth.

10. They will be delivered over to the power of
the sword;
     They will be a prey for foxes.

11. But the king will rejoice in God;
     Everyone who swears by Him will glory,
     For the mouths of those who speak lies
will be stopped.

Psalm 64

1. Hear my voice, O God, in my complaint;
    Preserve my life from dread of the
enemy.

2. Hide me from the secret counsel of evildoers,
    From the tumult of those who do
iniquity,

3. Who have sharpened their tongue like a
sword.
    They aimed bitter speech as their arrow,

4. To shoot from concealment at the blameless;
    Suddenly they shoot at him, and do not
fear.

5. They hold fast to themselves an evil purpose;
    They talk of laying snares secretly;
    They say, "Who can see them?"

6. They devise injustices, saying,
    "We are ready with a well-conceived
plot";
    For the inward thought and the heart of
a man are deep.

7. But God will shoot at them with an arrow;
Suddenly they will be wounded.

8. So they will make him stumble;
Their own tongue is against them;
All who see them will shake the head.

9. Then all men will fear,
And they will declare the work of God,
And will consider what He has done.

10. The righteous man will be glad in the LORD
and will take refuge in Him;
And all the upright in heart will glory.

Psalm 65

1. There will be silence before You, and praise
in Zion, O God,
And to You the vow will be performed.

2. O You who hear prayer,
To You all men come.

3. Iniquities prevail against me;
As for our transgressions, You forgive
them.

4. How blessed is the one whom You choose and bring near to You
> To dwell in Your courts.
> We will be satisfied with the goodness of Your house,
> Your holy temple.

5. By awesome deeds You answer us in righteousness, O God of our salvation,
> You who are the trust of all the ends of the earth and of the farthest sea;

6. Who establishes the mountains by His strength,
> Being girded with might;

7. Who stills the roaring of the seas,
> The roaring of their waves,
> And the tumult of the peoples.

8. They who dwell in the ends of the earth stand in awe of Your signs;
> You make the dawn and the sunset shout for joy.

9. You visit the earth and cause it to overflow;
> You greatly enrich it;
> The stream of God is full of water;

You prepare their grain, for thus You prepare the earth.

10. You water its furrows abundantly,
    You settle its ridges,
    You soften it with showers,
    You bless its growth.

11. You have crowned the year with Your bounty,
    And Your paths drip with fatness.

12. The pastures of the wilderness drip,
    And the hills gird themselves with rejoicing.

13. The meadows are clothed with flocks
    And the valleys are covered with grain;
    They shout for joy, yes, they sing.

Psalm 66

1. Shout joyfully to God, all the earth;

2. Sing the glory of His name;
    Make His praise glorious.

3. Say to God, "How awesome are Your works!
     Because of the greatness of Your power
Your enemies will give feigned obedience to
You.

4. "All the earth will worship You,
     And will sing praises to You;
     They will sing praises to Your name."

5. Come and see the works of God,
     Who is awesome in His deeds toward
the sons of men.

6. He turned the sea into dry land;
     They passed through the river on foot;
     There let us rejoice in Him!

7. He rules by His might forever;
     His eyes keep watch on the nations;
     Let not the rebellious exalt themselves.

8. Bless our God, O peoples,
     And sound His praise abroad,

9. Who keeps us in life
     And does not allow our feet to slip.

10. For You have tried us, O God;
     You have refined us as silver is refined.

11. You brought us into the net;
 	You laid an oppressive burden upon our loins.

12. You made men ride over our heads;
 	We went through fire and through water,
 	Yet You brought us out into a place of abundance.

13. I shall come into Your house with burnt offerings;
 	I shall pay You my vows,

14. Which my lips uttered
 	And my mouth spoke when I was in distress.

15. I shall offer to You burnt offerings of fat beasts,
 	With the smoke of rams;
 	I shall make an offering of bulls with male goats.

16. Come and hear, all who fear God,
 	And I will tell of what He has done for my soul.

17. I cried to Him with my mouth,
     And He was extolled with my tongue.

18. If I regard wickedness in my heart,
     The Lord will not hear;

19. But certainly God has heard;
     He has given heed to the voice of my
prayer.

20. Blessed be God,
     Who has not turned away my prayer
     Nor His lovingkindness from me.

Psalm 67

1. God be gracious to us and bless us,
    And cause His face to shine upon us—

2. That Your way may be known on the earth,
    Your salvation among all nations.

3. Let the peoples praise You, O God;
    Let all the peoples praise You.

4. Let the nations be glad and sing for joy;
    For You will judge the peoples with

uprightness
> And guide the nations on the earth.

5. Let the peoples praise You, O God;
> Let all the peoples praise You.

6. The earth has yielded its produce;
> God, our God, blesses us.

7. God blesses us,
> That all the ends of the earth may fear
Him.

Psalm 68

1. Let God arise, let His enemies be scattered,
> And let those who hate Him flee before
Him.

2. As smoke is driven away, so drive them
away;
> As wax melts before the fire,
> *So* let the wicked perish before God.

3. But let the righteous be glad; let them exult
before God;
> Yes, let them rejoice with gladness.

4. Sing to God, sing praises to His name;

> Lift up a song for Him who rides through the deserts,

> Whose name is the LORD, and exult before Him.

5. A father of the fatherless and a judge for the widows,

> Is God in His holy habitation.

6. God makes a home for the lonely;

> He leads out the prisoners into prosperity,

> Only the rebellious dwell in a parched land.

7. O God, when You went forth before Your people,

> When You marched through the wilderness,

8. The earth quaked;

> The heavens also dropped rain at the presence of God;

> Sinai itself quaked at the presence of God, the God of Israel.

9. You shed abroad a plentiful rain, O God;
     You confirmed Your inheritance when it
was parched.

10. Your creatures settled in it;
     You provided in Your goodness for the
poor, O God.

11. The Lord gives the command;
     The women who proclaim the *good*
tidings are a great host:

12. "Kings of armies flee, they flee,
     And she who remains at home will
divide the spoil!"

13. When you lie down among the sheepfolds,
     You are like the wings of a dove covered
with silver,
     And its pinions with glistening gold.

14. When the Almighty scattered the kings
there,
     It was snowing in Zalmon.

15. A mountain of God is the mountain of
Bashan;

A mountain of many peaks is the mountain of Bashan.

16. Why do you look with envy, O mountains with many peaks,
    At the mountain which God has desired for His abode?
    Surely the LORD will dwell there forever.

17. The chariots of God are myriads, thousands upon thousands;
    The Lord is among them as at Sinai, in holiness.

18. You have ascended on high, You have led captive Your captives;
    You have received gifts among men,
    Even among the rebellious also, that the LORD God may dwell there.

19. Blessed be the Lord, who daily bears our burden,
    The God who is our salvation.

20. God is to us a God of deliverances;
    And to GOD the Lord belong escapes from death.

21. Surely God will shatter the head of His enemies,

The hairy crown of him who goes on in his guilty deeds.

22. The Lord said, "I will bring them back from Bashan.

I will bring them back from the depths of the sea;

23. That your foot may shatter them in blood,

The tongue of your dogs may have its portion from your enemies."

24. They have seen Your procession, O God,

The procession of my God, my King, into the sanctuary.

25. The singers went on, the musicians after them,

In the midst of the maidens beating tambourines.

26. Bless God in the congregations,

Even the LORD, you who are of the fountain of Israel.

27. There is Benjamin, the youngest, ruling them,
> The princes of Judah *in* their throng,
> The princes of Zebulun, the princes of Naphtali.

28. Your God has commanded your strength;
> Show Yourself strong, O God, who have acted on our behalf.

29. Because of Your temple at Jerusalem
> Kings will bring gifts to You.

30. Rebuke the beasts in the reeds,
> The herd of bulls with the calves of the peoples,
> Trampling underfoot the pieces of silver;
> He has scattered the peoples who delight in war.

31. Envoys will come out of Egypt;
> Ethiopia will quickly stretch out her hands to God.

32. Sing to God, O kingdoms of the earth,
> Sing praises to the Lord,

33. To Him who rides upon the highest heavens, which are from ancient times;
>Behold, He speaks forth with His voice, a mighty voice.

34. Ascribe strength to God;
>His majesty is over Israel
>And His strength is in the skies.

35. O God, You are awesome from Your sanctuary.
>The God of Israel Himself gives strength and power to the people.
>Blessed be God!

Psalm 69

1. Save me, O God,
>For the waters have threatened my life.

2. I have sunk in deep mire, and there is no foothold;
>I have come into deep waters, and a flood overflows me.

3. I am weary with my crying; my throat is parched;

My eyes fail while I wait for my God.

4. Those who hate me without a cause are more than the hairs of my head;

Those who would destroy me are powerful, being wrongfully my enemies;

What I did not steal, I then have to restore.

5. O God, it is You who knows my folly,

And my wrongs are not hidden from You.

6. May those who wait for You not be ashamed through me, O Lord GOD of hosts;

May those who seek You not be dishonored through me, O God of Israel,

7. Because for Your sake I have borne reproach;

Dishonor has covered my face.

8. I have become estranged from my brothers

And an alien to my mother's sons.

9. For zeal for Your house has consumed me,
     And the reproaches of those who
reproach You have fallen on me.

10. When I wept in my soul with fasting,
     It became my reproach.

11. When I made sackcloth my clothing,
     I became a byword to them.

12. Those who sit in the gate talk about me,
     And I am the song of the drunkards.

13. But as for me, my prayer is to You, O
LORD, at an acceptable time;
     O God, in the greatness of Your
lovingkindness,
     Answer me with Your saving truth.

14. Deliver me from the mire and do not let me
sink;
     May I be delivered from my foes and
from the deep waters.

15. May the flood of water not overflow me
     Nor the deep swallow me up,
     Nor the pit shut its mouth on me.

16. Answer me, O LORD, for Your lovingkindness is good;
　　According to the greatness of Your compassion, turn to me,

17. And do not hide Your face from Your servant,
　　For I am in distress; answer me quickly.

18. Oh draw near to my soul and redeem it;
　　Ransom me because of my enemies!

19. You know my reproach and my shame and my dishonor;
　　All my adversaries are before You.

20. Reproach has broken my heart and I am so sick.
　　And I looked for sympathy, but there was none,
　　And for comforters, but I found none.

21. They also gave me gall for my food
　　And for my thirst they gave me vinegar to drink.

22. May their table before them become a snare;
      And when they are in peace, may it
become a trap.

23. May their eyes grow dim so that they
cannot see,
      And make their loins shake continually.

24. Pour out Your indignation on them,
      And may Your burning anger overtake
them.

25. May their camp be desolate;
      May none dwell in their tents.

26. For they have persecuted him whom You
Yourself have smitten,
      And they tell of the pain of those whom
You have wounded.

27. Add iniquity to their iniquity,
      And may they not come into Your
righteousness.

28. May they be blotted out of the book of life
      And may they not be recorded with the
righteous.

29. But I am afflicted and in pain;
    May Your salvation, O God, set me
securely on high.

30. I will praise the name of God with song
    And magnify Him with thanksgiving.

31. And it will please the LORD better than an
ox
    Or a young bull with horns and hoofs.

32. The humble have seen it and are glad;
    You who seek God, let your heart revive.

33. For the LORD hears the needy
    And does not despise His who are
prisoners.

34. Let heaven and earth praise Him,
    The seas and everything that moves in
them.

35. For God will save Zion and build the cities
of Judah,
    That they may dwell there and possess
it.

36. The descendants of His servants will inherit
it,

And those who love His name will dwell in it.

Psalm 70

1. O God, hasten to deliver me;
    O LORD, hasten to my help!

2. Let those be ashamed and humiliated
    Who seek my life;
    Let those be turned back and dishonored
    Who delight in my hurt.

3. Let those be turned back because of their shame
    Who say, "Aha, aha!"

4. Let all who seek You rejoice and be glad in You;
    And let those who love Your salvation say continually,
    "Let God be magnified."

5. But I am afflicted and needy;
    Hasten to me, O God!
    You are my help and my deliverer;
    O LORD, do not delay.

Psalm 71

1. In You, O LORD, I have taken refuge;
    Let me never be ashamed.

2. In Your righteousness deliver me and rescue me;
    Incline Your ear to me and save me.

3. Be to me a rock of habitation to which I may continually come;
    You have given commandment to save me,
    For You are my rock and my fortress.

4. Rescue me, O my God, out of the hand of the wicked,
    Out of the grasp of the wrongdoer and ruthless man,

5. For You are my hope;
    O Lord GOD, You are my confidence from my youth.

6. By You I have been sustained from my birth;
    You are He who took me from my mother's womb;
    My praise is continually of You.

7. I have become a marvel to many,
     For You are my strong refuge.

8. My mouth is filled with Your praise
     And with Your glory all day long.

9. Do not cast me off in the time of old age;
     Do not forsake me when my strength
fails.

10. For my enemies have spoken against me;
     And those who watch for my life have
consulted together,

11. Saying, "God has forsaken him;
     Pursue and seize him, for there is no one
to deliver."

12. O God, do not be far from me;
     O my God, hasten to my help!

13. Let those who are adversaries of my soul be
ashamed and consumed;
     Let them be covered with reproach and
dishonor, who seek to injure me.

14. But as for me, I will hope continually,
     And will praise You yet more and more.

15. My mouth shall tell of Your righteousness
   And of Your salvation all day long;
   For I do not know the sum of them.

16. I will come with the mighty deeds of the
Lord GOD;
   I will make mention of Your
righteousness, Yours alone.

17. O God, You have taught me from my youth,
   And I still declare Your wondrous
deeds.

18. And even when I am old and gray, O God,
do not forsake me,
   Until I declare Your strength to this
generation,
   Your power to all who are to come.

19. For Your righteousness, O God, reaches to
the heavens,
   You who have done great things;
   O God, who is like You?

20. You who have shown me many troubles
and distresses
   Will revive me again,

And will bring me up again from the depths of the earth.

21. May You increase my greatness
     And turn *to* comfort me.

22. I will also praise You with a harp,
     Even Your truth, O my God;
     To You I will sing praises with the lyre,
     O Holy One of Israel.

23. My lips will shout for joy when I sing praises to You;
     And my soul, which You have redeemed.

24. My tongue also will utter Your righteousness all day long;
     For they are ashamed, for they are humiliated who seek my hurt.

Psalm 72

1. Give the king Your judgments, O God,
      And Your righteousness to the king's
son.

2. May he judge Your people with
righteousness
      And Your afflicted with justice.

3. Let the mountains bring peace to the people,
      And the hills, in righteousness.

4. May he vindicate the afflicted of the people,
      Save the children of the needy
      And crush the oppressor.

5. Let them fear You while the sun endures,
      And as long as the moon, throughout all
generations.

6. May he come down like rain upon the mown
grass,
      Like showers that water the earth.

7. In his days may the righteous flourish,
      And abundance of peace till the moon is
no more.

8. May he also rule from sea to sea
	And from the River to the ends of the earth.

9. Let the nomads of the desert bow before him,
	And his enemies lick the dust.

10. Let the kings of Tarshish and of the islands bring presents;
	The kings of Sheba and Seba offer gifts.

11. And let all kings bow down before him,
	All nations serve him.

12. For he will deliver the needy when he cries for help,
	The afflicted also, and him who has no helper.

13. He will have compassion on the poor and needy,
	And the lives of the needy he will save.

14. He will rescue their life from oppression and violence,
	And their blood will be precious in his sight;

15. So may he live, and may the gold of Sheba be given to him;

> And let them pray for him continually;
> Let them bless him all day long.

16. May there be abundance of grain in the earth on top of the mountains;

> Its fruit will wave like the cedars of Lebanon;
> And may those from the city flourish like vegetation of the earth.

17. May his name endure forever;

> May his name increase as long as the sun shines;
> And let men bless themselves by him;
> Let all nations call him blessed.

18. Blessed be the LORD God, the God of Israel,

> Who alone works wonders.

19. And blessed be His glorious name forever;

> And may the whole earth be filled with His glory.
> Amen, and Amen.

20. The prayers of David the son of Jesse are ended.

Psalm 73

1. Surely God is good to Israel,
    To those who are pure in heart!

2. But as for me, my feet came close to stumbling,
    My steps had almost slipped.

3. For I was envious of the arrogant
    As I saw the prosperity of the wicked.

4. For there are no pains in their death,
    And their body is fat.

5. They are not in trouble as other men,
    Nor are they plagued like mankind.

6. Therefore pride is their necklace;
    The garment of violence covers them.

7. Their eye bulges from fatness;
    The imaginations of their heart run riot.

8. They mock and wickedly speak of oppression;
    They speak from on high.

9. They have set their mouth against the heavens,
>And their tongue parades through the earth.

10. Therefore his people return to this place,
>And waters of abundance are drunk by them.

11. They say, "How does God know?
>And is there knowledge with the Most High?"

12. Behold, these are the wicked;
>And always at ease, they have increased in wealth.

13. Surely in vain I have kept my heart pure
>And washed my hands in innocence;

14. For I have been stricken all day long
>And chastened every morning.

15. If I had said, "I will speak thus,"
>Behold, I would have betrayed the generation of Your children.

16. When I pondered to understand this,
>It was troublesome in my sight

17. Until I came into the sanctuary of God;
     Then I perceived their end.

18. Surely You set them in slippery places;
     You cast them down to destruction.

19. How they are destroyed in a moment!
     They are utterly swept away by sudden
terrors!

20. Like a dream when one awakes,
     O Lord, when aroused, You will despise
their form.

21. When my heart was embittered
     And I was pierced within,

22. Then I was senseless and ignorant;
     I was like a beast before You.

23. Nevertheless I am continually with You;
     You have taken hold of my right hand.

24. With Your counsel You will guide me,
     And afterward receive me to glory.

25. Whom have I in heaven but You?
     And besides You, I desire nothing on
earth.

26. My flesh and my heart may fail,
    But God is the strength of my heart and
my portion forever.

27. For, behold, those who are far from You
will perish;
    You have destroyed all those who are
unfaithful to You.

28. But as for me, the nearness of God is my
good;
    I have made the Lord GOD my refuge,
    That I may tell of all Your works.

Psalm 74

1. O God, why have You rejected us forever?
    Why does Your anger smoke against the
sheep of Your pasture?

2. Remember Your congregation, which You
have purchased of old,
    Which You have redeemed to be the
tribe of Your inheritance;
    And this Mount Zion, where You have
dwelt.

3. Turn Your footsteps toward the perpetual ruins;
   The enemy has damaged everything within the sanctuary.

4. Your adversaries have roared in the midst of Your meeting place;
   They have set up their own standards for signs.

5. It seems as if one had lifted up
   His axe in a forest of trees.

6. And now all its carved work
   They smash with hatchet and hammers.

7. They have burned Your sanctuary to the ground;
   They have defiled the dwelling place of Your name.

8. They said in their heart, "Let us completely subdue them."
   They have burned all the meeting places of God in the land.

9. We do not see our signs;
   There is no longer any prophet,

Nor is there any among us who knows how long.

10. How long, O God, will the adversary revile,
      And the enemy spurn Your name forever?

11. Why do You withdraw Your hand, even Your right hand?
      From within Your bosom, destroy them!

12. Yet God is my king from of old,
      Who works deeds of deliverance in the midst of the earth.

13. You divided the sea by Your strength;
      You broke the heads of the sea monsters in the waters.

14. You crushed the heads of Leviathan;
      You gave him as food for the creatures of the wilderness.

15. You broke open springs and torrents;
      You dried up ever-flowing streams.

16. Yours is the day, Yours also is the night;
      You have prepared the light and the sun.

17. You have established all the boundaries of the earth;
>You have made summer and winter.

18. Remember this, O LORD, that the enemy has reviled,
>And a foolish people has spurned Your name.

19. Do not deliver the soul of Your turtledove to the wild beast;
>Do not forget the life of Your afflicted forever.

20. Consider the covenant;
>For the dark places of the land are full of the habitations of violence.

21. Let not the oppressed return dishonored;
>Let the afflicted and needy praise Your name.

22. Arise, O God, and plead Your own cause;
>Remember how the foolish man reproaches You all day long.

23. Do not forget the voice of Your adversaries,
       The uproar of those who rise against
You which ascends continually.

Psalm 75

1. We give thanks to You, O God, we give
thanks,
       For Your name is near;
       Men declare Your wondrous works.

2. "When I select an appointed time,
       It is I who judge with equity.

3. "The earth and all who dwell in it melt;
       It is I who have firmly set its pillars.

4. "I said to the boastful, 'Do not boast,'
       And to the wicked, 'Do not lift up the
horn;

5. Do not lift up your horn on high,
       Do not speak with insolent pride.'"

6. For not from the east, nor from the west,
       Nor from the desert comes exaltation;

7. But God is the Judge;
    He puts down one and exalts another.

8. For a cup is in the hand of the LORD, and the wine foams;
    It is well mixed, and He pours out of this;
    Surely all the wicked of the earth must drain and drink down its dregs.

9. But as for me, I will declare it forever;
    I will sing praises to the God of Jacob.

10. And all the horns of the wicked He will cut off,
    But the horns of the righteous will be lifted up.

Psalm 76

1. God is known in Judah;
    His name is great in Israel.

2. His tabernacle is in Salem;
    His dwelling place also is in Zion.

3. There He broke the flaming arrows,
    The shield and the sword and the
weapons of war.

4. You are resplendent,
    More majestic than the mountains of
prey.

5. The stouthearted were plundered,
    They sank into sleep;
    And none of the warriors could use his
hands.

6. At Your rebuke, O God of Jacob,
    Both rider and horse were cast into a
dead sleep.

7. You, even You, are to be feared;
    And who may stand in Your presence
when once You are angry?

8. You caused judgment to be heard from
heaven;
    The earth feared and was still;

9. When God arose to judgment,
    To save all the humble of the earth.

10. For the wrath of man shall praise You;
   With a remnant of wrath You will gird
Yourself.

11. Make vows to the LORD your God and
fulfill them;
   Let all who are around Him bring gifts
to Him who is to be feared.

12. He will cut off the spirit of princes;
   He is feared by the kings of the earth.

Psalm 77

1. My voice rises to God, and I will cry aloud;
   My voice rises to God, and He will hear
me.

2. In the day of my trouble I sought the Lord;
   In the night my hand was stretched out
without weariness;
   My soul refused to be comforted.

3. When I remember God, then I am disturbed;
   When I sigh, then my spirit grows faint.

4. You have held my eyelids open;
    I am so troubled that I cannot speak.

5. I have considered the days of old,
    The years of long ago.

6. I will remember my song in the night;
    I will meditate with my heart,
    And my spirit ponders:

7. Will the Lord reject forever?
    And will He never be favorable again?

8. Has His lovingkindness ceased forever?
    Has His promise come to an end
forever?

9. Has God forgotten to be gracious,
    Or has He in anger withdrawn His
compassion?

10. Then I said, "It is my grief,
    That the right hand of the Most High has
changed."

11. I shall remember the deeds of the LORD;
    Surely I will remember Your wonders of
old.

12. I will meditate on all Your work
       And muse on Your deeds.

13. Your way, O God, is holy;
       What god is great like our God?

14. You are the God who works wonders;
       You have made known Your strength
among the peoples.

15. You have by Your power redeemed Your
people,
       The sons of Jacob and Joseph.

16. The waters saw You, O God;
       The waters saw You, they were in
anguish;
       The deeps also trembled.

17. The clouds poured out water;
       The skies gave forth a sound;
       Your arrows flashed here and there.

18. The sound of Your thunder was in the
whirlwind;
       The lightnings lit up the world;
       The earth trembled and shook.

19. Your way was in the sea
    And Your paths in the mighty waters,
    And Your footprints may not be known.

20. You led Your people like a flock
    By the hand of Moses and Aaron.

Psalm 78

1. Listen, O my people, to my instruction;
    Incline your ears to the words of my
mouth.

2. I will open my mouth in a parable;
    I will utter dark sayings of old,

3. Which we have heard and known,
    And our fathers have told us.

4. We will not conceal them from their children,
    But tell to the generation to come the
praises of the LORD,
    And His strength and His wondrous
works that He has done.

5. For He established a testimony in Jacob
    And appointed a law in Israel,

Which He commanded our fathers
    That they should teach them to their
children,

6. That the generation to come might know,
even the children yet to be born,
    That they may arise and tell them to
their children,

7. That they should put their confidence in God
        And not forget the works of God,
        But keep His commandments,

8. And not be like their fathers,
        A stubborn and rebellious generation,
        A generation that did not prepare its
heart
        And whose spirit was not faithful to
God.

9. The sons of Ephraim were archers equipped
with bows,
        Yet they turned back in the day of battle.

10. They did not keep the covenant of God
        And refused to walk in His law;

11. They forgot His deeds
    And His miracles that He had shown them.

12. He wrought wonders before their fathers
    In the land of Egypt, in the field of Zoan.

13. He divided the sea and caused them to pass through,
    And He made the waters stand up like a heap.

14. Then He led them with the cloud by day
    And all the night with a light of fire.

15. He split the rocks in the wilderness
    And gave them abundant drink like the ocean depths.

16. He brought forth streams also from the rock
    And caused waters to run down like rivers.

17. Yet they still continued to sin against Him,
    To rebel against the Most High in the desert.

18. And in their heart they put God to the test
    By asking food according to their desire.

19. Then they spoke against God;
  They said, "Can God prepare a table in
the wilderness?

20. "Behold, He struck the rock so that waters
gushed out,
  And streams were overflowing;
  Can He give bread also?
  Will He provide meat for His people?"

21. Therefore the LORD heard and was full of
wrath;
  And a fire was kindled against Jacob
  And anger also mounted against Israel,

22. Because they did not believe in God
  And did not trust in His salvation.

23. Yet He commanded the clouds above
  And opened the doors of heaven;

24. He rained down manna upon them to eat
  And gave them food from heaven.

25. Man did eat the bread of angels;
  He sent them food in abundance.

26. He caused the east wind to blow in the
heavens

And by His power He directed the south wind.

27. When He rained meat upon them like the dust,
Even winged fowl like the sand of the seas,

28. Then He let them fall in the midst of their camp,
Round about their dwellings.

29. So they ate and were well filled,
And their desire He gave to them.

30. Before they had satisfied their desire,
While their food was in their mouths,

31. The anger of God rose against them
And killed some of their stoutest ones,
And subdued the choice men of Israel.

32. In spite of all this they still sinned
And did not believe in His wonderful works.

33. So He brought their days to an end in futility
And their years in sudden terror.

34. When He killed them, then they sought Him,
>   And returned and searched diligently for God;

35. And they remembered that God was their rock,
>   And the Most High God their Redeemer.

36. But they deceived Him with their mouth
>   And lied to Him with their tongue.

37. For their heart was not steadfast toward Him,
>   Nor were they faithful in His covenant.

38. But He, being compassionate, forgave their iniquity and did not destroy them;
>   And often He restrained His anger
>   And did not arouse all His wrath.

39. Thus He remembered that they were but flesh,
>   A wind that passes and does not return.

40. How often they rebelled against Him in the wilderness
>   And grieved Him in the desert!

41. Again and again they tempted God,
       And pained the Holy One of Israel.

42. They did not remember His power,
       The day when He redeemed them from
the adversary,

43. When He performed His signs in Egypt
       And His marvels in the field of Zoan,

44. And turned their rivers to blood,
       And their streams, they could not drink.

45. He sent among them swarms of flies which
devoured them,
       And frogs which destroyed them.

46. He gave also their crops to the grasshopper
       And the product of their labor to the
locust.

47. He destroyed their vines with hailstones
       And their sycamore trees with frost.

48. He gave over their cattle also to the
hailstones
       And their herds to bolts of lightning.

49. He sent upon them His burning anger,
    Fury and indignation and trouble,
    A band of destroying angels.

50. He leveled a path for His anger;
    He did not spare their soul from death,
    But gave over their life to the plague,

51. And smote all the firstborn in Egypt,
    The first issue of their virility in the tents
of Ham.

52. But He led forth His own people like sheep
    And guided them in the wilderness like
a flock;

53. He led them safely, so that they did not fear;
    But the sea engulfed their enemies.

54. So He brought them to His holy land,
    To this hill country which His right hand
had gained.

55. He also drove out the nations before them
    And apportioned them for an
inheritance by measurement,
    And made the tribes of Israel dwell in
their tents.

56. Yet they tempted and rebelled against the Most High God
>
> And did not keep His testimonies,

57. But turned back and acted treacherously like their fathers;
>
> They turned aside like a treacherous bow.

58. For they provoked Him with their high places
>
> And aroused His jealousy with their graven images.

59. When God heard, He was filled with wrath
>
> And greatly abhorred Israel;

60. So that He abandoned the dwelling place at Shiloh,
>
> The tent which He had pitched among men,

61. And gave up His strength to captivity
>
> And His glory into the hand of the adversary.

62. He also delivered His people to the sword,
     And was filled with wrath at His
inheritance.

63. Fire devoured His young men,
     And His virgins had no wedding songs.

64. His priests fell by the sword,
     And His widows could not weep.

65. Then the Lord awoke as if from sleep,
     Like a warrior overcome by wine.

66. He drove His adversaries backward;
     He put on them an everlasting reproach.

67. He also rejected the tent of Joseph,
     And did not choose the tribe of Ephraim,

68. But chose the tribe of Judah,
     Mount Zion which He loved.

69. And He built His sanctuary like the heights,
     Like the earth which He has founded
forever.

70. He also chose David His servant
     And took him from the sheepfolds;

71. From the care of the ewes with suckling lambs He brought him
>   To shepherd Jacob His people,
>   And Israel His inheritance.

72. So he shepherded them according to the integrity of his heart,
>   And guided them with his skillful hands.

Psalm 79

1. O God, the nations have invaded Your inheritance;
>   They have defiled Your holy temple;
>   They have laid Jerusalem in ruins.

2. They have given the dead bodies of Your servants for food to the birds of the heavens,
>   The flesh of Your godly ones to the beasts of the earth.

3. They have poured out their blood like water round about Jerusalem;
>   And there was no one to bury them.

4. We have become a reproach to our neighbors,

A scoffing and derision to those around us.

5. How long, O LORD? Will You be angry forever?

Will Your jealousy burn like fire?

6. Pour out Your wrath upon the nations which do not know You,

And upon the kingdoms which do not call upon Your name.

7. For they have devoured Jacob

And laid waste his habitation.

8. Do not remember the iniquities of our forefathers against us;

Let Your compassion come quickly to meet us,

For we are brought very low.

9. Help us, O God of our salvation, for the glory of Your name;

And deliver us and forgive our sins for Your name's sake.

10. Why should the nations say, "Where is their God?"

Let there be known among the nations in our sight,

Vengeance for the blood of Your servants which has been shed.

11. Let the groaning of the prisoner come before You;

According to the greatness of Your power preserve those who are doomed to die.

12. And return to our neighbors sevenfold into their bosom

The reproach with which they have reproached You, O Lord.

13. So we Your people and the sheep of Your pasture

Will give thanks to You forever;

To all generations we will tell of Your praise.

Psalm 80

1. Oh, give ear, Shepherd of Israel,
>   You who lead Joseph like a flock;
>   You who are enthroned above the
cherubim, shine forth!

2. Before Ephraim and Benjamin and
Manasseh, stir up Your power
>   And come to save us!

3. O God, restore us
>   And cause Your face to shine upon us,
and we will be saved.

4. O LORD God of hosts,
>   How long will You be angry with the
prayer of Your people?

5. You have fed them with the bread of tears,
>   And You have made them to drink tears
in large measure.

6. You make us an object of contention to our
neighbors,
>   And our enemies laugh among
themselves.

7. O God of hosts, restore us

And cause Your face to shine upon us, and we will be saved.

8. You removed a vine from Egypt;

You drove out the nations and planted it.

9. You cleared the ground before it,

And it took deep root and filled the land.

10. The mountains were covered with its shadow,

And the cedars of God with its boughs.

11. It was sending out its branches to the sea

And its shoots to the River.

12. Why have You broken down its hedges,

So that all who pass that way pick its fruit?

13. A boar from the forest eats it away

And whatever moves in the field feeds on it.

14. O God of hosts, turn again now, we beseech You;

Look down from heaven and see, and take care of this vine,

15. Even the shoot which Your right hand has planted,
And on the son whom You have strengthened for Yourself.

16. It is burned with fire, it is cut down;
They perish at the rebuke of Your countenance.

17. Let Your hand be upon the man of Your right hand,
Upon the son of man whom You made strong for Yourself.

18. Then we shall not turn back from You;
Revive us, and we will call upon Your name.

19. O LORD God of hosts, restore us;
Cause Your face to shine upon us, and we will be saved.

Psalm 81

1. Sing for joy to God our strength;
    Shout joyfully to the God of Jacob.

2. Raise a song, strike the timbrel,
    The sweet sounding lyre with the harp.

3. Blow the trumpet at the new moon,
    At the full moon, on our feast day.

4. For it is a statute for Israel,
    An ordinance of the God of Jacob.

5. He established it for a testimony in Joseph
    When he went throughout the land of
Egypt.
    I heard a language that I did not know:

6. "I relieved his shoulder of the burden,
    His hands were freed from the basket.

7. "You called in trouble and I rescued you;
    I answered you in the hiding place of
thunder;
    I proved you at the waters of Meribah.

8. "Hear, O My people, and I will admonish you;
>   O Israel, if you would listen to Me!

9. "Let there be no strange god among you;
>   Nor shall you worship any foreign god.

10. "I, the LORD, am your God,
>   Who brought you up from the land of Egypt;
>   Open your mouth wide and I will fill it.

11. "But My people did not listen to My voice,
>   And Israel did not obey Me.

12. "So I gave them over to the stubbornness of their heart,
>   To walk in their own devices.

13. "Oh that My people would listen to Me,
>   That Israel would walk in My ways!

14. "I would quickly subdue their enemies
>   And turn My hand against their adversaries.

15. "Those who hate the LORD would pretend obedience to Him,

And their time of punishment would be forever.

16. "But I would feed you with the finest of the wheat,
And with honey from the rock I would satisfy you."

Psalm 82

1. God takes His stand in His own congregation;
He judges in the midst of the rulers.

2. How long will you judge unjustly
And show partiality to the wicked?

3. Vindicate the weak and fatherless;
Do justice to the afflicted and destitute.

4. Rescue the weak and needy;
Deliver them out of the hand of the wicked.

5. They do not know nor do they understand;
They walk about in darkness;

All the foundations of the earth are shaken.

6. I said, "You are gods,
>And all of you are sons of the Most High.

7. "Nevertheless you will die like men
>And fall like any one of the princes."

8. Arise, O God, judge the earth!
>For it is You who possesses all the nations.

Psalm 83

1. O God, do not remain quiet;
>Do not be silent and, O God, do not be still.

2. For behold, Your enemies make an uproar,
>And those who hate You have exalted themselves.

3. They make shrewd plans against Your people,
>And conspire together against Your treasured ones.

4. They have said, "Come, and let us wipe them out as a nation,

That the name of Israel be remembered no more."

5. For they have conspired together with one mind;

Against You they make a covenant:

6. The tents of Edom and the Ishmaelites,

Moab and the Hagrites;

7. Gebal and Ammon and Amalek,

Philistia with the inhabitants of Tyre;

8. Assyria also has joined with them;

They have become a help to the children of Lot.

9. Deal with them as with Midian,

As with Sisera and Jabin at the torrent of Kishon,

10. Who were destroyed at En-dor,

Who became as dung for the ground.

11. Make their nobles like Oreb and Zeeb

And all their princes like Zebah and Zalmunna,

12. Who said, "Let us possess for ourselves
    The pastures of God."

13. O my God, make them like the whirling dust,
    Like chaff before the wind.

14. Like fire that burns the forest
    And like a flame that sets the mountains on fire,

15. So pursue them with Your tempest
    And terrify them with Your storm.

16. Fill their faces with dishonor,
    That they may seek Your name, O LORD.

17. Let them be ashamed and dismayed forever,
    And let them be humiliated and perish,

18. That they may know that You alone, whose name is the LORD,
    Are the Most High over all the earth.

Psalm 84

1. How lovely are Your dwelling places,
      O LORD of hosts!

2. My soul longed and even yearned for the
courts of the LORD;
      My heart and my flesh sing for joy to the
living God.

3. The bird also has found a house,
      And the swallow a nest for herself,
where she may lay her young,
      Even Your altars, O LORD of hosts,
      My King and my God.

4. How blessed are those who dwell in Your
house!
      They are ever praising You.

5. How blessed is the man whose strength is in
You,
      In whose heart are the highways to Zion!

6. Passing through the valley of Baca they make
it a spring;
      The early rain also covers it with
blessings.

7. They go from strength to strength,
	Every one of them appears before God
in Zion.

8. O LORD God of hosts, hear my prayer;
	Give ear, O God of Jacob!

9. Behold our shield, O God,
	And look upon the face of Your
anointed.

10. For a day in Your courts is better than a
thousand outside.
	I would rather stand at the threshold of
the house of my God
	Than dwell in the tents of wickedness.

11. For the LORD God is a sun and shield;
	The LORD gives grace and glory;
	No good thing does He withhold from
those who walk uprightly.

12. O LORD of hosts,
	How blessed is the man who trusts in
You!

Psalm 85

1. O LORD, You showed favor to Your land;
    You restored the captivity of Jacob.

2. You forgave the iniquity of Your people;
    You covered all their sin.

3. You withdrew all Your fury;
        You turned away from Your burning
anger.

4. Restore us, O God of our salvation,
        And cause Your indignation toward us
to cease.

5. Will You be angry with us forever?
        Will You prolong Your anger to all
generations?

6. Will You not Yourself revive us again,
        That Your people may rejoice in You?

7. Show us Your lovingkindness, O LORD,
        And grant us Your salvation.

8. I will hear what God the LORD will say;
        For He will speak peace to His people, to

His godly ones;
   But let them not turn back to folly.

9. Surely His salvation is near to those who fear Him,
   That glory may dwell in our land.

10. Lovingkindness and truth have met together;
   Righteousness and peace have kissed each other.

11. Truth springs from the earth,
   And righteousness looks down from heaven.

12. Indeed, the LORD will give what is good,
   And our land will yield its produce.

13. Righteousness will go before Him
   And will make His footsteps into a way.

Psalm 86

1. Incline Your ear, O LORD, and answer me;
   For I am afflicted and needy.

2. Preserve my soul, for I am a godly man;
   O You my God, save Your servant who
trusts in You.

3. Be gracious to me, O Lord,
   For to You I cry all day long.

4. Make glad the soul of Your servant,
   For to You, O Lord, I lift up my soul.

5. For You, Lord, are good, and ready to
forgive,
   And abundant in lovingkindness to all
who call upon You.

6. Give ear, O LORD, to my prayer;
   And give heed to the voice of my
supplications!

7. In the day of my trouble I shall call upon
You,
   For You will answer me.

8. There is no one like You among the gods, O Lord,
> Nor are there any works like Yours.

9. All nations whom You have made shall come and worship before You, O Lord,
> And they shall glorify Your name.

10. For You are great and do wondrous deeds;
> You alone are God.

11. Teach me Your way, O LORD;
> I will walk in Your truth;
> Unite my heart to fear Your name.

12. I will give thanks to You, O Lord my God, with all my heart,
> And will glorify Your name forever.

13. For Your lovingkindness toward me is great,
> And You have delivered my soul from the depths of Sheol.

14. O God, arrogant men have risen up against me,
> And a band of violent men have sought

my life,
> And they have not set You before them.

15. But You, O Lord, are a God merciful and gracious,
> Slow to anger and abundant in lovingkindness and truth.

16. Turn to me, and be gracious to me;
> Oh grant Your strength to Your servant,
> And save the son of Your handmaid.

17. Show me a sign for good,
> That those who hate me may see *it* and be ashamed,
> Because You, O LORD, have helped me and comforted me.

Psalm 87

1. His foundation is in the holy mountains.

2. The LORD loves the gates of Zion
> More than all the other dwelling places of Jacob.

3. Glorious things are spoken of you,
 O city of God.

4. "I shall mention Rahab and Babylon among
those who know Me;
 Behold, Philistia and Tyre with Ethiopia:
 'This one was born there.'"

5. But of Zion it shall be said, "This one and
that one were born in her";
 And the Most High Himself will
establish her.

6. The LORD will count when He registers the
peoples,
 "This one was born there."

7. Then those who sing as well as those who
play the flutes shall say,
 "All my springs of joy are in you."

Psalm 88

1. O LORD, the God of my salvation,
  I have cried out by day and in the night before You.

2. Let my prayer come before You;
  Incline Your ear to my cry!

3. For my soul has had enough troubles,
  And my life has drawn near to Sheol.

4. I am reckoned among those who go down to the pit;
  I have become like a man without strength,

5. Forsaken among the dead,
  Like the slain who lie in the grave,
  Whom You remember no more,
  And they are cut off from Your hand.

6. You have put me in the lowest pit,
  In dark places, in the depths.

7. Your wrath has rested upon me,
  And You have afflicted me with all Your waves.

8. You have removed my acquaintances far from me;

    You have made me an object of loathing to them;

    I am shut up and cannot go out.

9. My eye has wasted away because of affliction;

    I have called upon You every day, O LORD;

    I have spread out my hands to You.

10. Will You perform wonders for the dead?

    Will the departed spirits rise and praise You?

11. Will Your lovingkindness be declared in the grave,

    Your faithfulness in Abaddon?

12. Will Your wonders be made known in the darkness?

    And Your righteousness in the land of forgetfulness?

13. But I, O LORD, have cried out to You for help,

And in the morning my prayer comes
before You.

14. O LORD, why do You reject my soul?
    Why do You hide Your face from me?

15. I was afflicted and about to die from my
youth on;
    I suffer Your terrors; I am overcome.

16. Your burning anger has passed over me;
    Your terrors have destroyed me.

17. They have surrounded me like water all day
long;
    They have encompassed me altogether.

18. You have removed lover and friend far
from me;
    My acquaintances are in darkness.

Psalm 89

1. I will sing of the lovingkindness of the LORD forever;
    To all generations I will make known Your faithfulness with my mouth.

2. For I have said, "Lovingkindness will be built up forever;
    In the heavens You will establish Your faithfulness."

3. "I have made a covenant with My chosen;
    I have sworn to David My servant,

4. I will establish your seed forever
    And build up your throne to all generations."

5. The heavens will praise Your wonders, O LORD;
    Your faithfulness also in the assembly of the holy ones.

6. For who in the skies is comparable to the LORD?
    Who among the sons of the mighty is like the LORD,

7. A God greatly feared in the council of the holy ones,

And awesome above all those who are around Him?

8. O LORD God of hosts, who is like You, O mighty LORD?

Your faithfulness also surrounds You.

9. You rule the swelling of the sea;

When its waves rise, You still them.

10. You Yourself crushed Rahab like one who is slain;

You scattered Your enemies with Your mighty arm.

11. The heavens are Yours, the earth also is Yours;

The world and all it contains, You have founded them.

12. The north and the south, You have created them;

Tabor and Hermon shout for joy at Your name.

13. You have a strong arm;
     Your hand is mighty, Your right hand is exalted.

14. Righteousness and justice are the foundation of Your throne;
     Lovingkindness and truth go before You.

15. How blessed are the people who know the joyful sound!
     O LORD, they walk in the light of Your countenance.

16. In Your name they rejoice all the day,
     And by Your righteousness they are exalted.

17. For You are the glory of their strength,
     And by Your favor our horn is exalted.

18. For our shield belongs to the LORD,
     And our king to the Holy One of Israel.

19. Once You spoke in vision to Your godly ones,
     And said, "I have given help to one who is mighty;

I have exalted one chosen from the people.

20. "I have found David My servant;
     With My holy oil I have anointed him,

21. With whom My hand will be established;
     My arm also will strengthen him.

22. "The enemy will not deceive him,
     Nor the son of wickedness afflict him.

23. "But I shall crush his adversaries before him,
     And strike those who hate him.

24. "My faithfulness and My lovingkindness will be with him,
     And in My name his horn will be exalted.

25. "I shall also set his hand on the sea
     And his right hand on the rivers.

26. "He will cry to Me, 'You are my Father,
     My God, and the rock of my salvation.'

27. "I also shall make him *My* firstborn,
     The highest of the kings of the earth.

28. "My lovingkindness I will keep for him forever,
And My covenant shall be confirmed to him.

29. "So I will establish his descendants forever
And his throne as the days of heaven.

30. "If his sons forsake My law
And do not walk in My judgments,

31. If they violate My statutes
And do not keep My commandments,

32. Then I will punish their transgression with the rod
And their iniquity with stripes.

33. "But I will not break off My lovingkindness from him,
Nor deal falsely in My faithfulness.

34. "My covenant I will not violate,
Nor will I alter the utterance of My lips.

35. "Once I have sworn by My holiness;
I will not lie to David.

36. "His descendants shall endure forever
    And his throne as the sun before Me.

37. "It shall be established forever like the
moon,
    And the witness in the sky is faithful."

38. But You have cast off and rejected,
    You have been full of wrath against
Your anointed.

39. You have spurned the covenant of Your
servant;
    You have profaned his crown in the
dust.

40. You have broken down all his walls;
    You have brought his strongholds to
ruin.

41. All who pass along the way plunder him;
    He has become a reproach to his
neighbors.

42. You have exalted the right hand of his
adversaries;
    You have made all his enemies rejoice.

43. You also turn back the edge of his sword
   And have not made him stand in battle.

44. You have made his splendor to cease
   And cast his throne to the ground.

45. You have shortened the days of his youth;
   You have covered him with shame.

46. How long, O LORD?
   Will You hide Yourself forever?
   Will Your wrath burn like fire?

47. Remember what my span of life is;
   For what vanity You have created all the
sons of men!

48. What man can live and not see death?
   Can he deliver his soul from the power
of Sheol?

49. Where are Your former loving kindnesses,
O Lord,
   Which You swore to David in Your
faithfulness?

50. Remember, O Lord, the reproach of Your
servants;

How I bear in my bosom the reproach of all the many peoples,

51. With which Your enemies have reproached, O LORD,
    With which they have reproached the footsteps of Your anointed.

52. Blessed be the LORD forever!
    Amen and Amen.

Psalm 90

1. Lord, You have been our dwelling place in all generations.

2. Before the mountains were born
    Or You gave birth to the earth and the world,
    Even from everlasting to everlasting, You are God.

3. You turn man back into dust
    And say, "Return, O children of men."

4. For a thousand years in Your sight
     Are like yesterday when it passes by,
     Or *as* a watch in the night.

5. You have swept them away like a flood, they fall asleep;
     In the morning they are like grass which sprouts anew.

6. In the morning it flourishes and sprouts anew;
     Toward evening it fades and withers away.

7. For we have been consumed by Your anger
     And by Your wrath we have been dismayed.

8. You have placed our iniquities before You,
     Our secret sins in the light of Your presence.

9. For all our days have declined in Your fury;
     We have finished our years like a sigh.

10. As for the days of our life, they contain seventy years,
     Or if due to strength, eighty years,

Yet their pride is but labor and sorrow;
For soon it is gone and we fly away.

11. Who understands the power of Your anger
And Your fury, according to the fear that
is due You?

12. So teach us to number our days,
That we may present to You a heart of
wisdom.

13. Do return, O LORD; how long will it be?
And be sorry for Your servants.

14. O satisfy us in the morning with Your
lovingkindness,
That we may sing for joy and be glad all
our days.

15. Make us glad according to the days You
have afflicted us,
And the years we have seen evil.

16. Let Your work appear to Your servants
And Your majesty to their children.

17. Let the favor of the Lord our God be upon
us;
And confirm for us the work of our

hands;

 Yes, confirm the work of our hands.

Psalm 91

1. He who dwells in the shelter of the Most High
 Will abide in the shadow of the Almighty.

2. I will say to the LORD, "My refuge and my fortress,
 My God, in whom I trust!"

3. For it is He who delivers you from the snare of the trapper
 And from the deadly pestilence.

4. He will cover you with His pinions,
 And under His wings you may seek refuge;
 His faithfulness is a shield and bulwark.

5. You will not be afraid of the terror by night,
 Or of the arrow that flies by day;

6. Of the pestilence that stalks in darkness,
    Or of the destruction that lays waste at
noon.

7. A thousand may fall at your side
    And ten thousand at your right hand,
    But it shall not approach you.

8. You will only look on with your eyes
    And see the recompense of the wicked.

9. For you have made the LORD, my refuge,
    Even the Most High, your dwelling
place.

10. No evil will befall you,
    Nor will any plague come near your
tent.

11. For He will give His angels charge
concerning you,
    To guard you in all your ways.

12. They will bear you up in their hands,
    That you do not strike your foot against
a stone.

13. You will tread upon the lion and cobra,
     The young lion and the serpent you will
trample down.

14. "Because he has loved Me, therefore I will
deliver him;
     I will set him securely on high, because
he has known My name.

15. "He will call upon Me, and I will answer
him;
     I will be with him in trouble;
     I will rescue him and honor him.

16. "With a long life I will satisfy him
     And let him see My salvation."

Psalm 92

1. It is good to give thanks to the LORD
     And to sing praises to Your name, O
Most High;

2. To declare Your lovingkindness in the
morning
     And Your faithfulness by night,

3. With the ten-stringed lute and with the harp,
  With resounding music upon the lyre.

4. For You, O LORD, have made me glad by what You have done,
  I will sing for joy at the works of Your hands.

5. How great are Your works, O LORD!
  Your thoughts are very deep.

6. A senseless man has no knowledge,
  Nor does a stupid man understand this:

7. That when the wicked sprouted up like grass
  And all who did iniquity flourished,
  It was only that they might be destroyed forevermore.

8. But You, O LORD, are on high forever.

9. For, behold, Your enemies, O LORD,
  For, behold, Your enemies will perish;
  All who do iniquity will be scattered.

10. But You have exalted my horn like that of the wild ox;
  I have been anointed with fresh oil.

11. And my eye has looked exultantly upon my foes,
> My ears hear of the evildoers who rise up against me.

12. The righteous man will flourish like the palm tree,
> He will grow like a cedar in Lebanon.

13. Planted in the house of the LORD,
> They will flourish in the courts of our God.

14. They will still yield fruit in old age;
> They shall be full of sap and very green,

15. To declare that the LORD is upright;
> He is my rock, and there is no unrighteousness in Him.

Psalm 93

1. The LORD reigns, He is clothed with majesty;
> The LORD has clothed and girded Himself with strength;

Indeed, the world is firmly established,
it will not be moved.

2. Your throne is established from of old;
    You are from everlasting.

3. The floods have lifted up, O LORD,
    The floods have lifted up their voice,
    The floods lift up their pounding waves.

4. More than the sounds of many waters,
    Than the mighty breakers of the sea,
    The LORD on high is mighty.

5. Your testimonies are fully confirmed;
    Holiness befits Your house,
    O LORD, forevermore.

Psalm 94

1. O LORD, God of vengeance,
    God of vengeance, shine forth!

2. Rise up, O Judge of the earth,
    Render recompense to the proud.

3. How long shall the wicked, O LORD,
    How long shall the wicked exult?

4. They pour forth words, they speak arrogantly;
> All who do wickedness vaunt themselves.

5. They crush Your people, O LORD,
> And afflict Your heritage.

6. They slay the widow and the stranger
> And murder the orphans.

7. They have said, "The LORD does not see,
> Nor does the God of Jacob pay heed."

8. Pay heed, you senseless among the people;
> And when will you understand, stupid ones?

9. He who planted the ear, does He not hear?
> He who formed the eye, does He not see?

10. He who chastens the nations, will He not rebuke,
> Even He who teaches man knowledge?

11. The LORD knows the thoughts of man,
> That they are a mere breath.

12. Blessed is the man whom You chasten, O LORD,

> And whom You teach out of Your law;

13. That You may grant him relief from the days of adversity,

> Until a pit is dug for the wicked.

14. For the LORD will not abandon His people,

> Nor will He forsake His inheritance.

15. For judgment will again be righteous,

> And all the upright in heart will follow
it.

16. Who will stand up for me against evildoers?

> Who will take his stand for me against
those who do wickedness?

17. If the LORD had not been my help,

> My soul would soon have dwelt in the
abode of silence.

18. If I should say, "My foot has slipped,"

> Your lovingkindness, O LORD, will hold
me up.

19. When my anxious thoughts multiply within me,

> Your consolations delight my soul.

20. Can a throne of destruction be allied with You,

> One which devises mischief by decree?

21. They band themselves together against the life of the righteous

> And condemn the innocent to death.

22. But the LORD has been my stronghold,

> And my God the rock of my refuge.

23. He has brought back their wickedness upon them

> And will destroy them in their evil;
> The LORD our God will destroy them.

Psalm 95

1. O come, let us sing for joy to the LORD,
     Let us shout joyfully to the rock of our salvation.

2. Let us come before His presence with thanksgiving,
     Let us shout joyfully to Him with psalms.

3. For the LORD is a great God
     And a great King above all gods,

4. In whose hand are the depths of the earth,
     The peaks of the mountains are His also.

5. The sea is His, for it was He who made it,
     And His hands formed the dry land.

6. Come, let us worship and bow down,
     Let us kneel before the LORD our Maker.

7. For He is our God,
     And we are the people of His pasture and the sheep of His hand.
     Today, if you would hear His voice,

8. Do not harden your hearts, as at Meribah,
As in the day of Massah in the wilderness,

9. "When your fathers tested Me,
They tried Me, though they had seen My work.

10. "For forty years I loathed that generation,
And said they are a people who err in their heart,
And they do not know My ways.

11. "Therefore I swore in My anger,
Truly they shall not enter into My rest."

Psalm 96

1. Sing to the LORD a new song;
Sing to the LORD, all the earth.

2. Sing to the LORD, bless His name;
Proclaim good tidings of His salvation from day to day.

3. Tell of His glory among the nations,
	His wonderful deeds among all the peoples.

4. For great is the LORD and greatly to be praised;
	He is to be feared above all gods.

5. For all the gods of the peoples are idols,
	But the LORD made the heavens.

6. Splendor and majesty are before Him,
	Strength and beauty are in His sanctuary.

7. Ascribe to the LORD, O families of the peoples,
	Ascribe to the LORD glory and strength.

8. Ascribe to the LORD the glory of His name;
	Bring an offering and come into His courts.

9. Worship the LORD in holy attire;
	Tremble before Him, all the earth.

10. Say among the nations, "The LORD reigns;
	Indeed, the world is firmly established,

it will not be moved;
>He will judge the peoples with equity."

11. Let the heavens be glad, and let the earth rejoice;
>Let the sea roar, and all it contains;

12. Let the field exult, and all that is in it.
>Then all the trees of the forest will sing for joy

13. Before the LORD, for He is coming,
>For He is coming to judge the earth.
>He will judge the world in righteousness
>And the peoples in His faithfulness.

Psalm 97

1. The LORD reigns, let the earth rejoice;
>Let the many islands be glad.

2. Clouds and thick darkness surround Him;
>Righteousness and justice are the foundation of His throne.

3. Fire goes before Him
    And burns up His adversaries round about.

4. His lightnings lit up the world;
    The earth saw and trembled.

5. The mountains melted like wax at the presence of the LORD,
    At the presence of the Lord of the whole earth.

6. The heavens declare His righteousness,
    And all the peoples have seen His glory.

7. Let all those be ashamed who serve graven images,
    Who boast themselves of idols;
    Worship Him, all you gods.

8. Zion heard this and was glad,
    And the daughters of Judah have rejoiced
    Because of Your judgments, O LORD.

9. For You are the LORD Most High over all the earth;
    You are exalted far above all gods.

10. Hate evil, you who love the LORD,
    Who preserves the souls of His godly
ones;
    He delivers them from the hand of the
wicked.

11. Light is sown like seed for the righteous
    And gladness for the upright in heart.

12. Be glad in the LORD, you righteous ones,
    And give thanks to His holy name.

Psalm 98

1. O sing to the LORD a new song,
    For He has done wonderful things,
    His right hand and His holy arm have
gained the victory for Him.

2. The LORD has made known His salvation;
    He has revealed His righteousness in the
sight of the nations.

3. He has remembered His lovingkindness and
His faithfulness to the house of Israel;
    All the ends of the earth have seen the
salvation of our God.

4. Shout joyfully to the LORD, all the earth;
    Break forth and sing for joy and sing praises.

5. Sing praises to the LORD with the lyre,
    With the lyre and the sound of melody.

6. With trumpets and the sound of the horn
    Shout joyfully before the King, the LORD.

7. Let the sea roar and all it contains,
    The world and those who dwell in it.

8. Let the rivers clap their hands,
    Let the mountains sing together for joy

9. Before the LORD, for He is coming to judge the earth;
    He will judge the world with righteousness
    And the peoples with equity.

Psalm 99

1. The LORD reigns, let the peoples tremble;
        He is enthroned above the cherubim, let
the earth shake!

2. The LORD is great in Zion,
        And He is exalted above all the peoples.

3. Let them praise Your great and awesome
name;
        Holy is He.

4. The strength of the King loves justice;
        You have established equity;
        You have executed justice and
righteousness in Jacob.

5. Exalt the LORD our God
        And worship at His footstool;
        Holy is He.

6. Moses and Aaron were among His priests,
        And Samuel was among those who
called on His name;
        They called upon the LORD and He
answered them.

7. He spoke to them in the pillar of cloud;
    They kept His testimonies
    And the statute that He gave them.

8. O LORD our God, You answered them;
    You were a forgiving God to them,
    And *yet* an avenger of their *evil* deeds.

9. Exalt the LORD our God
    And worship at His holy hill,
    For holy is the LORD our God.

Psalm 100

1. Shout joyfully to the LORD, all the earth.

2. Serve the LORD with gladness;
    Come before Him with joyful singing.

3. Know that the LORD Himself is God;
    It is He who has made us, and not we
ourselves;
    We are His people and the sheep of His
pasture.

4. Enter His gates with thanksgiving
And His courts with praise.
Give thanks to Him, bless His name.

5. For the LORD is good;
His lovingkindness is everlasting
And His faithfulness to all generations.

Psalm 101

1. I will sing of lovingkindness and justice,
To You, O LORD, I will sing praises.

2. I will give heed to the blameless way.
When will You come to me?
I will walk within my house in the
integrity of my heart.

3. I will set no worthless thing before my eyes;
I hate the work of those who fall away;
It shall not fasten its grip on me.

4. A perverse heart shall depart from me;
I will know no evil.

5. Whoever secretly slanders his neighbor, him
I will destroy;

No one who has a haughty look and an arrogant heart will I endure.

6. My eyes shall be upon the faithful of the land, that they may dwell with me;
   He who walks in a blameless way is the one who will minister to me.

7. He who practices deceit shall not dwell within my house;
   He who speaks falsehood shall not maintain his position before me.

8. Every morning I will destroy all the wicked of the land,
   So as to cut off from the city of the LORD all those who do iniquity.

Psalm 102

1. Hear my prayer, O LORD!
   And let my cry for help come to You.

2. Do not hide Your face from me in the day of my distress;
   Incline Your ear to me;

In the day when I call answer me quickly.

3. For my days have been consumed in smoke,
    And my bones have been scorched like a hearth.

4. My heart has been smitten like grass and has withered away,
    Indeed, I forget to eat my bread.

5. Because of the loudness of my groaning
    My bones cling to my flesh.

6. I resemble a pelican of the wilderness;
    I have become like an owl of the waste places.

7. I lie awake,
    I have become like a lonely bird on a housetop.

8. My enemies have reproached me all day long;
    Those who deride me have used my name as a curse.

9. For I have eaten ashes like bread
    And mingled my drink with weeping

10. Because of Your indignation and Your wrath,

    For You have lifted me up and cast me away.

11. My days are like a lengthened shadow,
    And I wither away like grass.

12. But You, O LORD, abide forever,
    And Your name to all generations.

13. You will arise and have compassion on Zion;

    For it is time to be gracious to her,
    For the appointed time has come.

14. Surely Your servants find pleasure in her stones

    And feel pity for her dust.

15. So the nations will fear the name of the LORD

    And all the kings of the earth Your glory.

16. For the LORD has built up Zion;
    He has appeared in His glory.

17. He has regarded the prayer of the destitute
     And has not despised their prayer.

18. This will be written for the generation to come,
     That a people yet to be created may praise the LORD.

19. For He looked down from His holy height;
     From heaven the LORD gazed upon the earth,

20. To hear the groaning of the prisoner,
     To set free those who were doomed to death,

21. That men may tell of the name of the LORD in Zion
     And His praise in Jerusalem,

22. When the peoples are gathered together,
     And the kingdoms, to serve the LORD.

23. He has weakened my strength in the way;
     He has shortened my days.

24. I say, "O my God, do not take me away in the midst of my days,

Your years are throughout all generations.

25. "Of old You founded the earth,
And the heavens are the work of Your hands.

26. "Even they will perish, but You endure;
And all of them will wear out like a garment;
Like clothing You will change them and they will be changed.

27. "But You are the same,
And Your years will not come to an end.

28. "The children of Your servants will continue,
And their descendants will be established before You."

Psalm 103

1. Bless the LORD, O my soul,
	And all that is within me, bless His holy name.

2. Bless the LORD, O my soul,
	And forget none of His benefits;

3. Who pardons all your iniquities,
	Who heals all your diseases;

4. Who redeems your life from the pit,
	Who crowns you with lovingkindness and compassion;

5. Who satisfies your years with good things,
	So that your youth is renewed like the eagle.

6. The LORD performs righteous deeds
	And judgments for all who are oppressed.

7. He made known His ways to Moses,
	His acts to the sons of Israel.

8. The LORD is compassionate and gracious,
    Slow to anger and abounding in lovingkindness.

9. He will not always strive with us,
    Nor will He keep His anger forever.

10. He has not dealt with us according to our sins,
    Nor rewarded us according to our iniquities.

11. For as high as the heavens are above the earth,
    So great is His lovingkindness toward those who fear Him.

12. As far as the east is from the west,
    So far has He removed our transgressions from us.

13. Just as a father has compassion on his children,
    So the LORD has compassion on those who fear Him.

14. For He Himself knows our frame;
    He is mindful that we are but dust.

15. As for man, his days are like grass;
    As a flower of the field, so he flourishes.

16. When the wind has passed over it, it is no more,
    And its place acknowledges it no longer.

17. But the lovingkindness of the LORD is from everlasting to everlasting on those who fear Him,
    And His righteousness to children's children,

18. To those who keep His covenant
    And remember His precepts to do them.

19. The LORD has established His throne in the heavens,
    And His sovereignty rules over all.

20. Bless the LORD, you His angels,
    Mighty in strength, who perform His word,
    Obeying the voice of His word!

21. Bless the LORD, all you His hosts,
    You who serve Him, doing His will.

22. Bless the LORD, all you works of His,
   In all places of His dominion;
   Bless the LORD, O my soul!

Psalm 104

1. Bless the LORD, O my soul!
   O LORD my God, You are very great;
   You are clothed with splendor and
majesty,

2. Covering Yourself with light as with a cloak,
   Stretching out heaven like a tent curtain.

3. He lays the beams of His upper chambers in
the waters;
   He makes the clouds His chariot;
   He walks upon the wings of the wind;

4. He makes the winds His messengers,
   Flaming fire His ministers.

5. He established the earth upon its
foundations,
   So that it will not totter forever and ever.

6. You covered it with the deep as with a garment;
>The waters were standing above the mountains.

7. At Your rebuke they fled,
>At the sound of Your thunder they hurried away.

8. The mountains rose; the valleys sank down
>To the place which You established for them.

9. You set a boundary that they may not pass over,
>So that they will not return to cover the earth.

10. He sends forth springs in the valleys;
>They flow between the mountains;

11. They give drink to every beast of the field;
>The wild donkeys quench their thirst.

12. Beside them the birds of the heavens dwell;
>They lift up their voices among the branches.

13. He waters the mountains from His upper chambers;
> The earth is satisfied with the fruit of His works.

14. He causes the grass to grow for the cattle,
> And vegetation for the labor of man,
> So that he may bring forth food from the earth,

15. And wine which makes man's heart glad,
> So that he may make his face glisten with oil,
> And food which sustains man's heart.

16. The trees of the LORD drink their fill,
> The cedars of Lebanon which He planted,

17. Where the birds build their nests,
> And the stork, whose home is the fir trees.

18. The high mountains are for the wild goats;
> The cliffs are a refuge for the shephanim.

19. He made the moon for the seasons;
> The sun knows the place of its setting.

20. You appoint darkness and it becomes night,
      In which all the beasts of the forest
prowl about.

21. The young lions roar after their prey
      And seek their food from God.

22. When the sun rises they withdraw
      And lie down in their dens.

23. Man goes forth to his work
      And to his labor until evening.

24. O LORD, how many are Your works!
      In wisdom You have made them all;
      The earth is full of Your possessions.

25. There is the sea, great and broad,
      In which are swarms without number,
      Animals both small and great.

26. There the ships move along,
      And Leviathan, which You have formed
to sport in it.

27. They all wait for You
      To give them their food in due season.

28. You give to them, they gather it up;
     You open Your hand, they are satisfied
with good.

29. You hide Your face, they are dismayed;
     You take away their spirit, they expire
     And return to their dust.

30. You send forth Your Spirit, they are created;
     And You renew the face of the ground.

31. Let the glory of the LORD endure forever;
     Let the LORD be glad in His works;

32. He looks at the earth, and it trembles;
     He touches the mountains, and they
smoke.

33. I will sing to the LORD as long as I live;
     I will sing praise to my God while I have
my being.

34. Let my meditation be pleasing to Him;
     As for me, I shall be glad in the LORD.

35. Let sinners be consumed from the earth
     And let the wicked be no more.
     Bless the LORD, O my soul.
     Praise the LORD!

Psalm 105

1. Oh give thanks to the LORD, call upon His name;

Make known His deeds among the peoples.

2. Sing to Him, sing praises to Him;
Speak of all His wonders.

3. Glory in His holy name;
Let the heart of those who seek the LORD be glad.

4. Seek the LORD and His strength;
Seek His face continually.

5. Remember His wonders which He has done,
His marvels and the judgments uttered by His mouth,

6. O seed of Abraham, His servant,
O sons of Jacob, His chosen ones!

7. He is the LORD our God;
His judgments are in all the earth.

8. He has remembered His covenant forever,
    The word which He commanded to a
thousand generations,

9. The covenant which He made with
Abraham,
    And His oath to Isaac.

10. Then He confirmed it to Jacob for a statute,
    To Israel as an everlasting covenant,

11. Saying, "To you I will give the land of
Canaan
    As the portion of your inheritance,"

12. When they were only a few men in number,
    Very few, and strangers in it.

13. And they wandered about from nation to
nation,
    From one kingdom to another people.

14. He permitted no man to oppress them,
    And He reproved kings for their sakes:

15. "Do not touch My anointed ones,
    And do My prophets no harm."

16. And He called for a famine upon the land;
     He broke the whole staff of bread.

17. He sent a man before them,
     Joseph, who was sold as a slave.

18. They afflicted his feet with fetters,
     He himself was laid in irons;

19. Until the time that his word came to pass,
     The word of the LORD tested him.

20. The king sent and released him,
     The ruler of peoples, and set him free.

21. He made him lord of his house
     And ruler over all his possessions,

22. To imprison his princes at will,
     That he might teach his elders wisdom.

23. Israel also came into Egypt;
     Thus Jacob sojourned in the land of
Ham.

24. And He caused His people to be very
fruitful,
     And made them stronger than their
adversaries.

25. He turned their heart to hate His people,
        To deal craftily with His servants.

26. He sent Moses His servant,
        And Aaron, whom He had chosen.

27. They performed His wondrous acts among
them,
        And miracles in the land of Ham.

28. He sent darkness and made it dark;
        And they did not rebel against His
words.

29. He turned their waters into blood
        And caused their fish to die.

30. Their land swarmed with frogs
        Even in the chambers of their kings.

31. He spoke, and there came a swarm of flies
        And gnats in all their territory.

32. He gave them hail for rain,
        And flaming fire in their land.

33. He struck down their vines also and their
fig trees,
        And shattered the trees of their territory.

34. He spoke, and locusts came,
    And young locusts, even without number,

35. And ate up all vegetation in their land,
    And ate up the fruit of their ground.

36. He also struck down all the firstborn in their land,
    The first fruits of all their vigor.

37. Then He brought them out with silver and gold,
    And among His tribes there was not one who stumbled.

38. Egypt was glad when they departed,
    For the dread of them had fallen upon them.

39. He spread a cloud for a covering,
    And fire to illumine by night.

40. They asked, and He brought quail,
    And satisfied them with the bread of heaven.

41. He opened the rock and water flowed out;
    It ran in the dry places like a river.

42. For He remembered His holy word
     With Abraham His servant;

43. And He brought forth His people with joy,
     His chosen ones with a joyful shout.

44. He gave them also the lands of the nations,
     That they might take possession of the
fruit of the peoples' labor,

45. So that they might keep His statutes
     And observe His laws,
     Praise the LORD!

Psalm 106

1. Praise the LORD!
     Oh give thanks to the LORD, for He is
good;
     For His lovingkindness is everlasting.

2. Who can speak of the mighty deeds of the
LORD,
     Or can show forth all His praise?

3. How blessed are those who keep justice,
     Who practice righteousness at all times!

4. Remember me, O LORD, in Your favor toward Your people;
>Visit me with Your salvation,

5. That I may see the prosperity of Your chosen ones,
>That I may rejoice in the gladness of Your nation,
>That I may glory with Your inheritance.

6. We have sinned like our fathers,
>We have committed iniquity, we have behaved wickedly.

7. Our fathers in Egypt did not understand Your wonders;
>They did not remember Your abundant kindnesses,
>But rebelled by the sea, at the Red Sea.

8. Nevertheless He saved them for the sake of His name,
>That He might make His power known.

9. Thus He rebuked the Red Sea and it dried up,
>And He led them through the deeps, as through the wilderness.

10. So He saved them from the hand of the one who hated them,
And redeemed them from the hand of the enemy.

11. The waters covered their adversaries;
Not one of them was left.

12. Then they believed His words;
They sang His praise.

13. They quickly forgot His works;
They did not wait for His counsel,

14. But craved intensely in the wilderness,
And tempted God in the desert.

15. So He gave them their request,
But sent a wasting disease among them.

16. When they became envious of Moses in the camp,
And of Aaron, the holy one of the LORD,

17. The earth opened and swallowed up Dathan,
And engulfed the company of Abiram.

18. And a fire blazed up in their company;
     The flame consumed the wicked.

19. They made a calf in Horeb
     And worshiped a molten image.

20. Thus they exchanged their glory
     For the image of an ox that eats grass.

21. They forgot God their Savior,
     Who had done great things in Egypt,

22. Wonders in the land of Ham
     And awesome things by the Red Sea.

23. Therefore He said that He would destroy them,
     Had not Moses His chosen one stood in the breach before Him,
     To turn away His wrath from destroying *them.*

24. Then they despised the pleasant land;
     They did not believe in His word,

25. But grumbled in their tents;
     They did not listen to the voice of the LORD.

26. Therefore He swore to them
      That He would cast them down in the wilderness,

27. And that He would cast their seed among the nations
      And scatter them in the lands.

28. They joined themselves also to Baal-peor,
      And ate sacrifices offered to the dead.

29. Thus they provoked Him to anger with their deeds,
      And the plague broke out among them.

30. Then Phinehas stood up and interposed,
      And so the plague was stayed.

31. And it was reckoned to him for righteousness,
      To all generations forever.

32. They also provoked Him to wrath at the waters of Meribah,
      So that it went hard with Moses on their account;

33. Because they were rebellious against His Spirit,

>He spoke rashly with his lips.

34. They did not destroy the peoples,
>As the LORD commanded them,

35. But they mingled with the nations
>And learned their practices,

36. And served their idols,
>Which became a snare to them.

37. They even sacrificed their sons and their daughters to the demons,

38. And shed innocent blood,
>The blood of their sons and their daughters,
>Whom they sacrificed to the idols of Canaan;
>And the land was polluted with the blood.

39. Thus they became unclean in their practices,
>And played the harlot in their deeds.

40. Therefore the anger of the LORD was kindled against His people
>   And He abhorred His inheritance.

41. Then He gave them into the hand of the nations,
>   And those who hated them ruled over them.

42. Their enemies also oppressed them,
>   And they were subdued under their power.

43. Many times He would deliver them;
>   They, however, were rebellious in their counsel,
>   And *so* sank down in their iniquity.

44. Nevertheless He looked upon their distress
>   When He heard their cry;

45. And He remembered His covenant for their sake,
>   And relented according to the greatness of His lovingkindness.

46. He also made them *objects* of compassion
>   In the presence of all their captors.

47. Save us, O LORD our God,
     And gather us from among the nations,
     To give thanks to Your holy name
     And glory in Your praise.

48. Blessed be the LORD, the God of Israel,
     From everlasting even to everlasting.
     And let all the people say, "Amen."
     Praise the LORD!

Psalm 107

1. Oh give thanks to the LORD, for He is good,
     For His lovingkindness is everlasting.

2. Let the redeemed of the LORD say so,
     Whom He has redeemed from the hand
of the adversary

3. And gathered from the lands,
     From the east and from the west,
     From the north and from the south.

4. They wandered in the wilderness in a desert
region;
     They did not find a way to an inhabited
city.

5. They were hungry and thirsty;
     Their soul fainted within them.

6. Then they cried out to the LORD in their trouble;
     He delivered them out of their distresses.

7. He led them also by a straight way,
     To go to an inhabited city.

8. Let them give thanks to the LORD for His lovingkindness,
     And for His wonders to the sons of men!

9. For He has satisfied the thirsty soul,
     And the hungry soul He has filled with what is good.

10. There were those who dwelt in darkness and in the shadow of death,
     Prisoners in misery and chains,

11. Because they had rebelled against the words of God
     And spurned the counsel of the Most High.

12. Therefore He humbled their heart with labor;

They stumbled and there was none to help.

13. Then they cried out to the LORD in their trouble;

He saved them out of their distresses.

14. He brought them out of darkness and the shadow of death

And broke their bands apart.

15. Let them give thanks to the LORD for His lovingkindness,

And for His wonders to the sons of men!

16. For He has shattered gates of bronze

And cut bars of iron asunder.

17. Fools, because of their rebellious way,

And because of their iniquities, were afflicted.

18. Their soul abhorred all kinds of food,

And they drew near to the gates of death.

19. Then they cried out to the LORD in their trouble;

> He saved them out of their distresses.

20. He sent His word and healed them,

> And delivered them from their destructions.

21. Let them give thanks to the LORD for His lovingkindness,

> And for His wonders to the sons of men!

22. Let them also offer sacrifices of thanksgiving,

> And tell of His works with joyful singing.

23. Those who go down to the sea in ships,

> Who do business on great waters;

24. They have seen the works of the LORD,

> And His wonders in the deep.

25. For He spoke and raised up a stormy wind,

> Which lifted up the waves of the sea.

26. They rose up to the heavens, they went down to the depths;

> Their soul melted away in their misery.

27. They reeled and staggered like a drunken man,

>   And were at their wits' end.

28. Then they cried to the LORD in their trouble,

>   And He brought them out of their distresses.

29. He caused the storm to be still,

>   So that the waves of the sea were hushed.

30. Then they were glad because they were quiet,

>   So He guided them to their desired haven.

31. Let them give thanks to the LORD for His lovingkindness,

>   And for His wonders to the sons of men!

32. Let them extol Him also in the congregation of the people,

>   And praise Him at the seat of the elders.

33. He changes rivers into a wilderness
And springs of water into a thirsty
ground;

34. A fruitful land into a salt waste,
Because of the wickedness of those who
dwell in it.

35. He changes a wilderness into a pool of
water
And a dry land into springs of water;

36. And there He makes the hungry to dwell,
So that they may establish an inhabited
city,

37. And sow fields and plant vineyards,
And gather a fruitful harvest.

38. Also He blesses them and they multiply
greatly,
And He does not let their cattle decrease.

39. When they are diminished and bowed
down
Through oppression, misery and sorrow,

40. He pours contempt upon princes
>And makes them wander in a pathless waste.

41. But He sets the needy securely on high away from affliction,
>And makes his families like a flock.

42. The upright see it and are glad;
>But all unrighteousness shuts its mouth.

43. Who is wise? Let him give heed to these things,
>And consider the loving kindnesses of the LORD.

Psalm 108

1. My heart is steadfast, O God;
>I will sing, I will sing praises, even with my soul.

2. Awake, harp and lyre;
>I will awaken the dawn!

3. I will give thanks to You, O LORD, among the peoples,

And I will sing praises to You among the nations.

4. For Your lovingkindness is great above the heavens,
> And Your truth reaches to the skies.

5. Be exalted, O God, above the heavens,
> And Your glory above all the earth.

6. That Your beloved may be delivered,
> Save with Your right hand, and answer me!

7. God has spoken in His holiness:
> "I will exult, I will portion out Shechem
> And measure out the valley of Succoth.

8. "Gilead is Mine, Manasseh is Mine;
> Ephraim also is the helmet of My head;
> Judah is My scepter.

9. "Moab is My washbowl;
> Over Edom I shall throw My shoe;
> Over Philistia I will shout aloud."

10. Who will bring me into the besieged city?
> Who will lead me to Edom?

11. Have not You Yourself, O God, rejected us?
    And will You not go forth with our
armies, O God?

12. Oh give us help against the adversary,
    For deliverance by man is in vain.

13. Through God we will do valiantly,
    And it is He who shall tread down our
adversaries.

Psalm 109

1. O God of my praise,
    Do not be silent!

2. For they have opened the wicked and
deceitful mouth against me;
    They have spoken against me with a
lying tongue.

3. They have also surrounded me with words
of hatred,
    And fought against me without cause.

4. In return for my love they act as my accusers;
    But I am in prayer.

5. Thus they have repaid me evil for good
   And hatred for my love.

6. Appoint a wicked man over him,
   And let an accuser stand at his right hand.

7. When he is judged, let him come forth guilty,
   And let his prayer become sin.

8. Let his days be few;
   Let another take his office.

9. Let his children be fatherless
   And his wife a widow.

10. Let his children wander about and beg;
    And let them seek sustenance far from their ruined homes.

11. Let the creditor seize all that he has,
    And let strangers plunder the product of his labor.

12. Let there be none to extend lovingkindness to him,
    Nor any to be gracious to his fatherless children.

13. Let his posterity be cut off;
In a following generation let their name be blotted out.

14. Let the iniquity of his fathers be remembered before the LORD,
And do not let the sin of his mother be blotted out.

15. Let them be before the LORD continually,
That He may cut off their memory from the earth;

16. Because he did not remember to show lovingkindness,
But persecuted the afflicted and needy man,
And the despondent in heart, to put them to death.

17. He also loved cursing, so it came to him;
And he did not delight in blessing, so it was far from him.

18. But he clothed himself with cursing as with his garment,
And it entered into his body like water
And like oil into his bones.

19. Let it be to him as a garment with which he covers himself,
>   And for a belt with which he constantly girds himself.

20. Let this be the reward of my accusers from the LORD,
>   And of those who speak evil against my soul.

21. But You, O GOD, the Lord, deal kindly with me for Your name's sake;
>   Because Your lovingkindness is good, deliver me;

22. For I am afflicted and needy,
>   And my heart is wounded within me.

23. I am passing like a shadow when it lengthens;
>   I am shaken off like the locust.

24. My knees are weak from fasting,
>   And my flesh has grown lean, without fatness.

25. I also have become a reproach to them;
>   When they see me, they wag their head.

26. Help me, O LORD my God;
  Save me according to Your
lovingkindness.

27. And let them know that this is Your hand;
  You, LORD, have done it.

28. Let them curse, but You bless;
  When they arise, they shall be ashamed,
  But Your servant shall be glad.

29. Let my accusers be clothed with dishonor,
  And let them cover themselves with
their own shame as with a robe.

30. With my mouth I will give thanks
abundantly to the LORD;
  And in the midst of many I will praise
Him.

31. For He stands at the right hand of the
needy,
  To save him from those who judge his
soul.

Psalm 110

1. The LORD says to my Lord:
    "Sit at My right hand
    Until I make Your enemies a footstool
for Your feet."

2. The LORD will stretch forth Your strong
scepter from Zion, saying,
    "Rule in the midst of Your enemies."

3. Your people will volunteer freely in the day
of Your power;
    In holy array, from the womb of the
dawn,
    Your youth are to You as the dew.

4. The LORD has sworn and will not change
His mind,
    "You are a priest forever
    According to the order of Melchizedek."

5. The Lord is at Your right hand;
    He will shatter kings in the day of His
wrath.

6. He will judge among the nations,
    He will fill them with corpses,

He will shatter the chief men over a broad country.

7. He will drink from the brook by the wayside;
Therefore He will lift up His head.

Psalm 111

1. Praise the LORD!
I will give thanks to the LORD with all my heart,
In the company of the upright and in the assembly.

2. Great are the works of the LORD;
They are studied by all who delight in them.

3. Splendid and majestic is His work,
And His righteousness endures forever.

4. He has made His wonders to be remembered;
The LORD is gracious and compassionate.

5. He has given food to those who fear Him;
    He will remember His covenant forever.

6. He has made known to His people the power of His works,
    In giving them the heritage of the nations.

7. The works of His hands are truth and justice;
    All His precepts are sure.

8. They are upheld forever and ever;
    They are performed in truth and uprightness.

9. He has sent redemption to His people;
    He has ordained His covenant forever;
    Holy and awesome is His name.

10. The fear of the LORD is the beginning of wisdom;
    A good understanding have all those who do His commandments;
    His praise endures forever.

Psalm 112

1. Praise the LORD!

How blessed is the man who fears the LORD,

Who greatly delights in His commandments.

2. His descendants will be mighty on earth;

The generation of the upright will be blessed.

3. Wealth and riches are in his house,

And his righteousness endures forever.

4. Light arises in the darkness for the upright;

He is gracious and compassionate and righteous.

5. It is well with the man who is gracious and lends;

He will maintain his cause in judgment.

6. For he will never be shaken;

The righteous will be remembered forever.

7. He will not fear evil tidings;
   His heart is steadfast, trusting in the
LORD.

8. His heart is upheld, he will not fear,
   Until he looks with satisfaction on his
adversaries.

9. He has given freely to the poor,
   His righteousness endures forever;
   His horn will be exalted in honor.

10. The wicked will see it and be vexed,
   He will gnash his teeth and melt away;
   The desire of the wicked will perish.

Psalm 113

1. Praise the LORD!
   Praise, O servants of the LORD,
   Praise the name of the LORD.

2. Blessed be the name of the LORD
   From this time forth and forever.

3. From the rising of the sun to its setting
   The name of the LORD is to be praised.

4. The LORD is high above all nations;
    His glory is above the heavens.

5. Who is like the LORD our God,
    Who is enthroned on high,

6. Who humbles Himself to behold
    The things that are in heaven and in the
earth?

7. He raises the poor from the dust
    And lifts the needy from the ash heap,

8. To make them sit with princes,
    With the princes of His people.

9. He makes the barren woman abide in the
house
    As a joyful mother of children.
    Praise the LORD!

Psalm 114

1. When Israel went forth from Egypt,
   The house of Jacob from a people of
strange language,

2. Judah became His sanctuary,
   Israel, His dominion.

3. The sea looked and fled;
   The Jordan turned back.

4. The mountains skipped like rams,
   The hills, like lambs.

5. What ails you, O sea, that you flee?
   O Jordan, that you turn back?

6. O mountains, that you skip like rams?
   O hills, like lambs?

7. Tremble, O earth, before the Lord,
   Before the God of Jacob,

8. Who turned the rock into a pool of water,
   The flint into a fountain of water.

Psalm 115

1. Not to us, O LORD, not to us,
    But to Your name give glory
    Because of Your lovingkindness, because
of Your truth.

2. Why should the nations say,
    "Where, now, is their God?"

3. But our God is in the heavens;
    He does whatever He pleases.

4. Their idols are silver and gold,
    The work of man's hands.

5. They have mouths, but they cannot speak;
    They have eyes, but they cannot see;

6. They have ears, but they cannot hear;
    They have noses, but they cannot smell;

7. They have hands, but they cannot feel;
    They have feet, but they cannot walk;
    They cannot make a sound with their
throat.

8. Those who make them will become like them,

> Everyone who trusts in them.

9. O Israel, trust in the LORD;

> He is their help and their shield.

10. O house of Aaron, trust in the LORD;

> He is their help and their shield.

11. You who fear the LORD, trust in the LORD;

> He is their help and their shield.

12. The LORD has been mindful of us; He will bless us;

> He will bless the house of Israel;
> He will bless the house of Aaron.

13. He will bless those who fear the LORD,

> The small together with the great.

14. May the LORD give you increase,

> You and your children.

15. May you be blessed of the LORD,

> Maker of heaven and earth.

16. The heavens are the heavens of the LORD,
　　But the earth He has given to the sons of
men.

17. The dead do not praise the LORD,
　　Nor *do* any who go down into silence;

18. But as for us, we will bless the LORD
　　From this time forth and forever.
　　Praise the LORD!

Psalm 116

1. I love the LORD, because He hears
　　My voice and my supplications.

2. Because He has inclined His ear to me,
　　Therefore I shall call upon Him as long
as I live.

3. The cords of death encompassed me
　　And the terrors of Sheol came upon me;
　　I found distress and sorrow.

4. Then I called upon the name of the LORD:
　　"O LORD, I beseech You, save my life!"

5. Gracious is the LORD, and righteous;
    Yes, our God is compassionate.

6. The LORD preserves the simple;
    I was brought low, and He saved me.

7. Return to your rest, O my soul,
    For the LORD has dealt bountifully with
you.

8. For You have rescued my soul from death,
    My eyes from tears,
    My feet from stumbling.

9. I shall walk before the LORD
    In the land of the living.

10. I believed when I said,
    "I am greatly afflicted."

11. I said in my alarm,
    "All men are liars."

12. What shall I render to the LORD
    For all His benefits toward me?

13. I shall lift up the cup of salvation
    And call upon the name of the LORD.

14. I shall pay my vows to the LORD,
      Oh may it be in the presence of all His people.

15. Precious in the sight of the LORD
      Is the death of His godly ones.

16. O LORD, surely I am Your servant,
      I am Your servant, the son of Your handmaid,
      You have loosed my bonds.

17. To You I shall offer a sacrifice of thanksgiving,
      And call upon the name of the LORD.

18. I shall pay my vows to the LORD,
      Oh may it be in the presence of all His people,

19. In the courts of the LORD'S house,
      In the midst of you, O Jerusalem.
      Praise the LORD!

Psalm 117

1. Praise the LORD, all nations;
      Laud Him, all peoples!

2. For His lovingkindness is great toward us,
      And the truth of the LORD is
everlasting.
      Praise the LORD!

Psalm 118

1. Give thanks to the LORD, for He is good;
      For His lovingkindness is everlasting.

2. Oh let Israel say,
      "His lovingkindness is everlasting."

3. Oh let the house of Aaron say,
      "His lovingkindness is everlasting."

4. Oh let those who fear the LORD say,
      "His lovingkindness is everlasting."

5. From my distress I called upon the LORD;
      The LORD answered me and set me in a
large place.

6. The LORD is for me; I will not fear;
    What can man do to me?

7. The LORD is for me among those who help me;
    Therefore I will look with satisfaction on those who hate me.

8. It is better to take refuge in the LORD
    Than to trust in man.

9. It is better to take refuge in the LORD
    Than to trust in princes.

10. All nations surrounded me;
    In the name of the LORD I will surely cut them off.

11. They surrounded me, yes, they surrounded me;
    In the name of the LORD I will surely cut them off.

12. They surrounded me like bees;
    They were extinguished as a fire of thorns;
    In the name of the LORD I will surely cut them off.

13. You pushed me violently so that I was falling,
> But the LORD helped me.

14. The LORD is my strength and song,
> And He has become my salvation.

15. The sound of joyful shouting and salvation is in the tents of the righteous;
> The right hand of the LORD does valiantly.

16. The right hand of the LORD is exalted;
> The right hand of the LORD does valiantly.

17. I will not die, but live,
> And tell of the works of the LORD.

18. The LORD has disciplined me severely,
> But He has not given me over to death.

19. Open to me the gates of righteousness;
> I shall enter through them, I shall give thanks to the LORD.

20. This is the gate of the LORD;
> The righteous will enter through it.

21. I shall give thanks to You, for You have answered me,
>   And You have become my salvation.

22. The stone which the builders rejected
>   Has become the chief corner stone.

23. This is the LORD'S doing;
>   It is marvelous in our eyes.

24. This is the day which the LORD has made;
>   Let us rejoice and be glad in it.

25. O LORD, do save, we beseech You;
>   O LORD, we beseech You, do send
prosperity!

26. Blessed is the one who comes in the name of the LORD;
>   We have blessed you from the house of the LORD.

27. The LORD is God, and He has given us light;
>   Bind the festival sacrifice with cords to
the horns of the altar.

28. You are my God, and I give thanks to You;
>   You are my God, I extol You.

29. Give thanks to the LORD, for He is good;
     For His lovingkindness is everlasting.

Psalm 119

1. How blessed are those whose way is blameless,
     Who walk in the law of the LORD.

2. How blessed are those who observe His testimonies,
     Who seek Him with all their heart.

3. They also do no unrighteousness;
     They walk in His ways.

4. You have ordained Your precepts,
     That we should keep them diligently.

5. Oh that my ways may be established
     To keep Your statutes!

6. Then I shall not be ashamed
     When I look upon all Your commandments.

7. I shall give thanks to You with uprightness of heart,
>
> When I learn Your righteous judgments.

8. I shall keep Your statutes;
>
> Do not forsake me utterly!

Beth.

9. How can a young man keep his way pure?
>
> By keeping it according to Your word.

10. With all my heart I have sought You;
>
> Do not let me wander from Your commandments.

11. Your word I have treasured in my heart,
>
> That I may not sin against You.

12. Blessed are You, O LORD;
>
> Teach me Your statutes.

13. With my lips I have told of
>
> All the ordinances of Your mouth.

14. I have rejoiced in the way of Your testimonies,

As much as in all riches.

15. I will meditate on Your precepts
And regard Your ways.

16. I shall delight in Your statutes;
I shall not forget Your word.

Gimel.

17. Deal bountifully with Your servant,
That I may live and keep Your word.

18. Open my eyes, that I may behold
Wonderful things from Your law.

19. I am a stranger in the earth;
Do not hide Your commandments from
me.

20. My soul is crushed with longing
After Your ordinances at all times.

21. You rebuke the arrogant, the cursed,
    Who wander from Your
commandments.

22. Take away reproach and contempt from me,
    For I observe Your testimonies.

23. Even though princes sit and talk against me,
    Your servant meditates on Your statutes.

24. Your testimonies also are my delight;
    They are my counselors.

Daleth.

25. My soul cleaves to the dust;
    Revive me according to Your word.

26. I have told of my ways, and You have
answered me;
    Teach me Your statutes.

27. Make me understand the way of Your
precepts,
    So I will meditate on Your wonders.

28. My soul weeps because of grief;
    Strengthen me according to Your word.

29. Remove the false way from me,
　　And graciously grant me Your law.

30. I have chosen the faithful way;
　　I have placed Your ordinances before
me.

31. I cling to Your testimonies;
　　O LORD, do not put me to shame!

32. I shall run the way of Your commandments,
　　For You will enlarge my heart.

He.

33. Teach me, O LORD, the way of Your
statutes,
　　And I shall observe it to the end.

34. Give me understanding, that I may observe
Your law
　　And keep it with all my heart.

35. Make me walk in the path of Your
commandments,
　　For I delight in it.

36. Incline my heart to Your testimonies
    And not to dishonest gain.

37. Turn away my eyes from looking at vanity,
    And revive me in Your ways.

38. Establish Your word to Your servant,
    As that which produces reverence for
You.

39. Turn away my reproach which I dread,
    For Your ordinances are good.

40. Behold, I long for Your precepts;
    Revive me through Your righteousness.

Vav.

41. May Your loving kindnesses also come to
me, O LORD,
    Your salvation according to Your word;

42. So I will have an answer for him who
reproaches me,
    For I trust in Your word.

43. And do not take the word of truth utterly out of my mouth,
>	For I wait for Your ordinances.

44. So I will keep Your law continually,
>	Forever and ever.

45. And I will walk at liberty,
>	For I seek Your precepts.

46. I will also speak of Your testimonies before kings
>	And shall not be ashamed.

47. I shall delight in Your commandments,
>	Which I love.

48. And I shall lift up my hands to Your commandments,
>	Which I love;
>	And I will meditate on Your statutes.

Zayin.

49. Remember the word to Your servant,
>	In which You have made me hope.

50. This is my comfort in my affliction,
     That Your word has revived me.

51. The arrogant utterly deride me,
     Yet I do not turn aside from Your law.

52. I have remembered Your ordinances from of old, O LORD,
     And comfort myself.

53. Burning indignation has seized me because of the wicked,
     Who forsake Your law.

54. Your statutes are my songs
     In the house of my pilgrimage.

55. O LORD, I remember Your name in the night,
     And keep Your law.

56. This has become mine,
     That I observe Your precepts.

Heth.

57. The LORD is my portion;
     I have promised to keep Your words.

58. I sought Your favor with all my heart;
    Be gracious to me according to Your word.

59. I considered my ways
    And turned my feet to Your testimonies.

60. I hastened and did not delay
    To keep Your commandments.

61. The cords of the wicked have encircled me,
    But I have not forgotten Your law.

62. At midnight I shall rise to give thanks to You
    Because of Your righteous ordinances.

63. I am a companion of all those who fear You,
    And of those who keep Your precepts.

64. The earth is full of Your lovingkindness, O LORD;
    Teach me Your statutes.

Teth.

65. You have dealt well with Your servant,
    O LORD, according to Your word.

66. Teach me good discernment and knowledge,
>For I believe in Your commandments.

67. Before I was afflicted I went astray,
>But now I keep Your word.

68. You are good and do good;
>Teach me Your statutes.

69. The arrogant have forged a lie against me;
>With all my heart I will observe Your precepts.

70. Their heart is covered with fat,
>But I delight in Your law.

71. It is good for me that I was afflicted,
>That I may learn Your statutes.

72. The law of Your mouth is better to me
>Than thousands of gold and silver pieces.

Yodh.

73. Your hands made me and fashioned me;

Give me understanding, that I may learn
Your commandments.

74. May those who fear You see me and be
glad,
　　Because I wait for Your word.

75. I know, O LORD, that Your judgments are
righteous,
　　And that in faithfulness You have
afflicted me.

76. O may Your lovingkindness comfort me,
　　According to Your word to Your
servant.

77. May Your compassion come to me that I
may live,
　　For Your law is my delight.

78. May the arrogant be ashamed, for they
subvert me with a lie;
　　But I shall meditate on Your precepts.

79. May those who fear You turn to me,
　　Even those who know Your testimonies.

80. May my heart be blameless in Your statutes,
　　So that I will not be ashamed.

Kaph.

81. My soul languishes for Your salvation;
      I wait for Your word.

82. My eyes fail with longing for Your word,
      While I say, "When will You comfort
me?"

83. Though I have become like a wineskin in
the smoke,
      I do not forget Your statutes.

84. How many are the days of Your servant?
      When will You execute judgment on
those who persecute me?

85. The arrogant have dug pits for me,
      Men who are not in accord with Your
law.

86. All Your commandments are faithful;
      They have persecuted me with a lie; help
me!

87. They almost destroyed me on earth,
      But as for me, I did not forsake Your
precepts.

88. Revive me according to Your lovingkindness,
    So that I may keep the testimony of Your mouth.

Lamedh.

89. Forever, O LORD,
    Your word is settled in heaven.

90. Your faithfulness continues throughout all generations;
    You established the earth, and it stands.

91. They stand this day according to Your ordinances,
    For all things are Your servants.

92. If Your law had not been my delight,
    Then I would have perished in my affliction.

93. I will never forget Your precepts,
    For by them You have revived me.

94. I am Yours, save me;
    For I have sought Your precepts.

95. The wicked wait for me to destroy me;
      I shall diligently consider Your
testimonies.

96. I have seen a limit to all perfection;
      Your commandment is exceedingly
broad.

Mem.

97. O how I love Your law!
      It is my meditation all the day.

98. Your commandments make me wiser than
my enemies,
      For they are ever mine.

99. I have more insight than all my teachers,
      For Your testimonies are my meditation.

100. I understand more than the aged,
      Because I have observed Your precepts.

101. I have restrained my feet from every evil
way,
      That I may keep Your word.

102. I have not turned aside from Your ordinances,
>
> For You Yourself have taught me.

103. How sweet are Your words to my taste!
>
> Yes, sweeter than honey to my mouth!

104. From Your precepts I get understanding;
>
> Therefore I hate every false way.

Nun.

105. Your word is a lamp to my feet
>
> And a light to my path.

106. I have sworn and I will confirm it,
>
> That I will keep Your righteous ordinances.

107. I am exceedingly afflicted;
>
> Revive me, O LORD, according to Your word.

108. O accept the freewill offerings of my mouth, O LORD,
>
> And teach me Your ordinances.

109. My life is continually in my hand,
       Yet I do not forget Your law.

110. The wicked have laid a snare for me,
       Yet I have not gone astray from Your
precepts.

111. I have inherited Your testimonies forever,
       For they are the joy of my heart.

112. I have inclined my heart to perform Your
statutes
       Forever, even to the end.

Samekh.

113. I hate those who are double-minded,
       But I love Your law.

114. You are my hiding place and my shield;
       I wait for Your word.

115. Depart from me, evildoers,
       That I may observe the commandments
of my God.

116. Sustain me according to Your word, that I
may live;

And do not let me be ashamed of my hope.

117. Uphold me that I may be safe,
    That I may have regard for Your statutes continually.

118. You have rejected all those who wander from Your statutes,
    For their deceitfulness is useless.

119. You have removed all the wicked of the earth like dross;
    Therefore I love Your testimonies.

120. My flesh trembles for fear of You,
    And I am afraid of Your judgments.

Ayin.

121. I have done justice and righteousness;
    Do not leave me to my oppressors.

122. Be surety for Your servant for good;
    Do not let the arrogant oppress me.

123. My eyes fail with longing for Your salvation
>   And for Your righteous word.

124. Deal with Your servant according to Your lovingkindness
>   And teach me Your statutes.

125. I am Your servant; give me understanding,
>   That I may know Your testimonies.

126. It is time for the LORD to act,
>   For they have broken Your law.

127. Therefore I love Your commandments
>   Above gold, yes, above fine gold.

128. Therefore I esteem right all Your precepts concerning everything,
>   I hate every false way.

Pe.

129. Your testimonies are wonderful;
>   Therefore my soul observes them.

130. The unfolding of Your words gives light;
>   It gives understanding to the simple.

131. I opened my mouth wide and panted,
    For I longed for Your commandments.

132. Turn to me and be gracious to me,
    After Your manner with those who love
Your name.

133. Establish my footsteps in Your word,
    And do not let any iniquity have
dominion over me.

134. Redeem me from the oppression of man,
    That I may keep Your precepts.

135. Make Your face shine upon Your servant,
    And teach me Your statutes.

136. My eyes shed streams of water,
    Because they do not keep Your law.

Tsadhe.

137. Righteous are You, O LORD,
    And upright are Your judgments.

138. You have commanded Your testimonies in
righteousness
    And exceeding faithfulness.

139. My zeal has consumed me,
Because my adversaries have forgotten
Your words.

140. Your word is very pure,
Therefore Your servant loves it.

141. I am small and despised,
Yet I do not forget Your precepts.

142. Your righteousness is an everlasting
righteousness,
And Your law is truth.

143. Trouble and anguish have come upon me,
Yet Your commandments are my
delight.

144. Your testimonies are righteous forever;
Give me understanding that I may live.

Qoph.

145. I cried with all my heart; answer me, O
LORD!
I will observe Your statutes.

146. I cried to You; save me
    And I shall keep Your testimonies.

147. I rise before dawn and cry for help;
    I wait for Your words.

148. My eyes anticipate the night watches,
    That I may meditate on Your word.

149. Hear my voice according to Your
lovingkindness;
    Revive me, O LORD, according to Your
ordinances.

150. Those who follow after wickedness draw
near;
    They are far from Your law.

151. You are near, O LORD,
    And all Your commandments are truth.

152. Of old I have known from Your
testimonies
    That You have founded them forever.

Resh.

153. Look upon my affliction and rescue me,
     For I do not forget Your law.

154. Plead my cause and redeem me;
     Revive me according to Your word.

155. Salvation is far from the wicked,
     For they do not seek Your statutes.

156. Great are Your mercies, O LORD;
     Revive me according to Your
ordinances.

157. Many are my persecutors and my
adversaries,
     Yet I do not turn aside from Your
testimonies.

158. I behold the treacherous and loathe them,
     Because they do not keep Your word.

159. Consider how I love Your precepts;
     Revive me, O LORD, according to Your
lovingkindness.

160. The sum of Your word is truth,
　　　And every one of Your righteous
ordinances is everlasting.

Shin.

161. Princes persecute me without cause,
　　　But my heart stands in awe of Your
words.

162. I rejoice at Your word,
　　　As one who finds great spoil.

163. I hate and despise falsehood,
　　　But I love Your law.

164. Seven times a day I praise You,
　　　Because of Your righteous ordinances.

165. Those who love Your law have great
peace,
　　　And nothing causes them to stumble.

166. I hope for Your salvation, O LORD,
　　　And do Your commandments.

167. My soul keeps Your testimonies,
　　　And I love them exceedingly.

168. I keep Your precepts and Your testimonies,
    For all my ways are before You.

Tav.

169. Let my cry come before You, O LORD;
    Give me understanding according to
Your word.

170. Let my supplication come before You;
    Deliver me according to Your word.

171. Let my lips utter praise,
    For You teach me Your statutes.

172. Let my tongue sing of Your word,
    For all Your commandments are
righteousness.

173. Let Your hand be ready to help me,
    For I have chosen Your precepts.

174. I long for Your salvation, O LORD,
    And Your law is my delight.

175. Let my soul live that it may praise You,
    And let Your ordinances help me.

176. I have gone astray like a lost sheep; seek Your servant,
    For I do not forget Your commandments.

Psalm 120

1. In my trouble I cried to the LORD,
    And He answered me.

2. Deliver my soul, O LORD, from lying lips,
    From a deceitful tongue.

3. What shall be given to you, and what more shall be done to you,
    You deceitful tongue?

4. Sharp arrows of the warrior,
    With the burning coals of the broom tree.

5. Woe is me, for I sojourn in Meshech,
    For I dwell among the tents of Kedar!

6. Too long has my soul had its dwelling
    With those who hate peace.

7. I am for peace, but when I speak,
    They are for war.

Psalm 121

1. I will lift up my eyes to the mountains;
    From where shall my help come?

2. My help comes from the LORD,
    Who made heaven and earth.

3. He will not allow your foot to slip;
    He who keeps you will not slumber.

4. Behold, He who keeps Israel
    Will neither slumber nor sleep.

5. The LORD is your keeper;
    The LORD is your shade on your right
hand.

6. The sun will not smite you by day,
    Nor the moon by night.

7. The LORD will protect you from all evil;
    He will keep your soul.

8. The LORD will guard your going out and your coming in
>From this time forth and forever.

Psalm 122

1. I was glad when they said to me,
"Let us go to the house of the LORD."

2. Our feet are standing
Within your gates, O Jerusalem,

3. Jerusalem, that is built
As a city that is compact together;

4. To which the tribes go up, even the tribes of the LORD—
An ordinance for Israel—
To give thanks to the name of the LORD.

5. For there thrones were set for judgment,
The thrones of the house of David.

6. Pray for the peace of Jerusalem:
"May they prosper who love you.

7. "May peace be within your walls,
And prosperity within your palaces."

8. For the sake of my brothers and my friends,
	I will now say, "May peace be within you."

9. For the sake of the house of the LORD our God,
	I will seek your good.

Psalm 123

1. To You I lift up my eyes,
	O You who are enthroned in the heavens!

2. Behold, as the eyes of servants look to the hand of their master,
	As the eyes of a maid to the hand of her mistress,
	So our eyes look to the LORD our God,
	Until He is gracious to us.

3. Be gracious to us, O LORD, be gracious to us,
	For we are greatly filled with contempt.

4. Our soul is greatly filled
	With the scoffing of those who are at

ease,
　　And with the contempt of the proud.

Psalm 124

1. "Had it not been the LORD who was on our side,"
　　Let Israel now say,

2. "Had it not been the LORD who was on our side
　　When men rose up against us,

3. Then they would have swallowed us alive,
　　When their anger was kindled against us;

4. Then the waters would have engulfed us,
　　The stream would have swept over our soul;

5. Then the raging waters would have swept over our soul."

6. Blessed be the LORD,
　　Who has not given us to be torn by their teeth.

7. Our soul has escaped as a bird out of the snare of the trapper;
The snare is broken and we have escaped.

8. Our help is in the name of the LORD,
Who made heaven and earth.

Psalm 125

1. Those who trust in the LORD
Are as Mount Zion, which cannot be moved but abides forever.

2. As the mountains surround Jerusalem,
So the LORD surrounds His people
From this time forth and forever.

3. For the scepter of wickedness shall not rest upon the land of the righteous,
So that the righteous will not put forth their hands to do wrong.

4. Do good, O LORD, to those who are good
And to those who are upright in their hearts.

5. But as for those who turn aside to their crooked ways,
The LORD will lead them away with the doers of iniquity.
Peace be upon Israel.

Psalm 126

1. When the LORD brought back the captive ones of Zion,
We were like those who dream.

2. Then our mouth was filled with laughter
And our tongue with joyful shouting;
Then they said among the nations,
"The LORD has done great things for them."

3. The LORD has done great things for us;
We are glad.

4. Restore our captivity, O LORD,
As the streams in the South.

5. Those who sow in tears shall reap with joyful shouting.

6. He who goes to and fro weeping, carrying his bag of seed,

Shall indeed come again with a shout of joy, bringing his sheaves with him.

Psalm 127

1. Unless the LORD builds the house,

They labor in vain who build it;
Unless the LORD guards the city,
The watchman keeps awake in vain.

2. It is vain for you to rise up early,

To retire late,
To eat the bread of painful labors;
For He gives to His beloved even in his sleep.

3. Behold, children are a gift of the LORD,

The fruit of the womb is a reward.

4. Like arrows in the hand of a warrior,

So are the children of one's youth.

5. How blessed is the man whose quiver is full of them;

They will not be ashamed

When they speak with their enemies in the gate.

Psalm 128

1. How blessed is everyone who fears the LORD,
    Who walks in His ways.

2. When you shall eat of the fruit of your hands,
    You will be happy and it will be well with you.

3. Your wife shall be like a fruitful vine
    Within your house,
    Your children like olive plants
    Around your table.

4. Behold, for thus shall the man be blessed
    Who fears the LORD.

5. The LORD bless you from Zion,
    And may you see the prosperity of Jerusalem all the days of your life.

6Indeed, may you see your children's children.
    Peace be upon Israel!

Psalm 129

1. "Many times they have persecuted me from my youth up,"
> Let Israel now say,

2. "Many times they have persecuted me from my youth up;
> Yet they have not prevailed against me.

3. "The plowers plowed upon my back;
> They lengthened their furrows."

4. The LORD is righteous;
> He has cut in two the cords of the wicked.

5. May all who hate Zion
> Be put to shame and turned backward;

6. Let them be like grass upon the housetops,
> Which withers before it grows up;

7. With which the reaper does not fill his hand,
> Or the binder of sheaves his bosom;

8. Nor do those who pass by say,
> "The blessing of the LORD be upon you;
> We bless you in the name of the LORD."

Psalm 130

1. Out of the depths I have cried to You, O
LORD.

2. Lord, hear my voice!
    Let Your ears be attentive
    To the voice of my supplications.

3. If You, LORD, should mark iniquities,
    O Lord, who could stand?

4. But there is forgiveness with You,
    That You may be feared.

5. I wait for the LORD, my soul does wait,
    And in His word do I hope.

6. My soul waits for the Lord
    More than the watchmen for the
morning;
    Indeed, more than the watchmen for the
morning.

7. O Israel, hope in the LORD;
    For with the LORD there is
lovingkindness,
    And with Him is abundant redemption.

8. And He will redeem Israel
   From all his iniquities.

Psalm 131

1. O LORD, my heart is not proud, nor my eyes haughty;
   Nor do I involve myself in great matters,
   Or in things too difficult for me.

2. Surely I have composed and quieted my soul;
   Like a weaned child rests against his mother,
   My soul is like a weaned child within me.

3. O Israel, hope in the LORD
   From this time forth and forever.

Psalm 132

1. Remember, O LORD, on David's behalf,
    All his affliction;

2. How he swore to the LORD
    And vowed to the Mighty One of Jacob,

3. "Surely I will not enter my house,
    Nor lie on my bed;

4. I will not give sleep to my eyes
    Or slumber to my eyelids,

5. Until I find a place for the LORD,
    A dwelling place for the Mighty One of
Jacob."

6. Behold, we heard of it in Ephrathah,
    We found it in the field of Jaar.

7. Let us go into His dwelling place;
    Let us worship at His footstool.

8. Arise, O LORD, to Your resting place,
    You and the ark of Your strength.

9. Let Your priests be clothed with righteousness,
>   And let Your godly ones sing for joy.

10. For the sake of David Your servant,
>   Do not turn away the face of Your anointed.

11. The LORD has sworn to David
>   A truth from which He will not turn back:
>   "Of the fruit of your body I will set upon your throne.

12. "If your sons will keep My covenant
>   And My testimony which I will teach them,
>   Their sons also shall sit upon your throne forever."

13. For the LORD has chosen Zion;
>   He has desired it for His habitation.

14. "This is My resting place forever;
>   Here I will dwell, for I have desired it.

15. "I will abundantly bless her provision;
>   I will satisfy her needy with bread.

16. "Her priests also I will clothe with salvation,
   And her godly ones will sing aloud for joy.

17. "There I will cause the horn of David to spring forth;
   I have prepared a lamp for Mine anointed.

18. "His enemies I will clothe with shame,
   But upon himself his crown shall shine."

Psalm 133

1. Behold, how good and how pleasant it is
   For brothers to dwell together in unity!

2. It is like the precious oil upon the head,
   Coming down upon the beard,
   Even Aaron's beard,
   Coming down upon the edge of his robes.

3. It is like the dew of Hermon
   Coming down upon the mountains of Zion;

For there the LORD commanded the blessing—life forever.

Psalm 134

1. Behold, bless the LORD, all servants of the LORD,
 Who serve by night in the house of the LORD!

2. Lift up your hands to the sanctuary
 And bless the LORD.

3. May the LORD bless you from Zion,
 He who made heaven and earth.

Psalm 135

1. Praise the LORD!
 Praise the name of the LORD;
 Praise Him, O servants of the LORD,

2. You who stand in the house of the LORD,
 In the courts of the house of our God!

3. Praise the LORD, for the LORD is good;
    Sing praises to His name, for it is lovely.

4. For the LORD has chosen Jacob for Himself,
    Israel for His own possession.

5. For I know that the LORD is great
    And that our Lord is above all gods.

6. Whatever the LORD pleases, He does,
    In heaven and in earth, in the seas and in
all deeps.

7. He causes the vapors to ascend from the
ends of the earth;
    Who makes lightnings for the rain,
    Who brings forth the wind from His
treasuries.

8. He smote the firstborn of Egypt,
    Both of man and beast.

9. He sent signs and wonders into your midst,
O Egypt,
    Upon Pharaoh and all his servants.

10. He smote many nations
    And slew mighty kings,

11. Sihon, king of the Amorites,
     And Og, king of Bashan,
     And all the kingdoms of Canaan;

12. And He gave their land as a heritage,
     A heritage to Israel His people.

13. Your name, O LORD, is everlasting,
     Your remembrance, O LORD,
throughout all generations.

14. For the LORD will judge His people
     And will have compassion on His
servants.

15. The idols of the nations are but silver and
gold,
     The work of man's hands.

16. They have mouths, but they do not speak;
     They have eyes, but they do not see;

17. They have ears, but they do not hear,
     Nor is there any breath at all in their
mouths.

18. Those who make them will be like them,
     Yes, everyone who trusts in them.

19. O house of Israel, bless the LORD;
       O house of Aaron, bless the LORD;

20. O house of Levi, bless the LORD;
       You who revere the LORD, bless the
LORD.

21. Blessed be the LORD from Zion,
       Who dwells in Jerusalem.
       Praise the LORD!

Psalm 136

1. Give thanks to the LORD, for He is good,
       For His lovingkindness is everlasting.

2. Give thanks to the God of gods,
       For His lovingkindness is everlasting.

3. Give thanks to the Lord of lords,
       For His lovingkindness is everlasting.

4. To Him who alone does great wonders,
       For His lovingkindness is everlasting;

5. To Him who made the heavens with skill,
       For His lovingkindness is everlasting;

6. To Him who spread out the earth above the waters,

    For His lovingkindness is everlasting;

7. To Him who made the great lights,

    For His lovingkindness is everlasting:

8. The sun to rule by day,

    For His lovingkindness is everlasting,

9. The moon and stars to rule by night,

    For His lovingkindness is everlasting.

10. To Him who smote the Egyptians in their firstborn,

    For His lovingkindness is everlasting,

11. And brought Israel out from their midst,

    For His lovingkindness is everlasting,

12. With a strong hand and an outstretched arm,

    For His lovingkindness is everlasting.

13. To Him who divided the Red Sea asunder,

    For His lovingkindness is everlasting,

14. And made Israel pass through the midst of it,

> For His lovingkindness is everlasting;

15. But He overthrew Pharaoh and his army in the Red Sea,

> For His lovingkindness is everlasting.

16. To Him who led His people through the wilderness,

> For His lovingkindness is everlasting;

17. To Him who smote great kings,

> For His lovingkindness is everlasting,

18. And slew mighty kings,

> For His lovingkindness is everlasting:

19. Sihon, king of the Amorites,

> For His lovingkindness is everlasting,

20. And Og, king of Bashan,

> For His lovingkindness is everlasting,

21. And gave their land as a heritage,

> For His lovingkindness is everlasting,

22. Even a heritage to Israel His servant,

> For His lovingkindness is everlasting.

23. Who remembered us in our low estate,
   For His lovingkindness is everlasting,

24. And has rescued us from our adversaries,
   For His lovingkindness is everlasting;

25. Who gives food to all flesh,
   For His lovingkindness is everlasting.

26. Give thanks to the God of heaven,
   For His lovingkindness is everlasting.

Psalm 137

1. By the rivers of Babylon,
   There we sat down and wept,
   When we remembered Zion.

2. Upon the willows in the midst of it
   We hung our harps.
3. For there are captors demanded of us
songs,
   And our tormentors mirth, saying,
   "Sing us one of the songs of Zion."

4. How can we sing the Lord's song
   In a foreign land?

5. If I forget you, O Jerusalem,
    May my right hand forget her skill.

6. May my tongue cling to the roof of my mouth
    If I do not remember you,
    If I do not exalt Jerusalem
    Above my chief joy.

7. Remember, O Lord, against the sons of Edom
    The day of Jerusalem,
    Who said, "Raze it, raze it
    To its very foundation."

8. O daughter of Babylon, you devastated one,
    How blessed will be the one who repays you with the recompense with which you have repaid us.
9. How blessed will be the one who seizes and dashes your little ones against the rock.

Psalm 138

1. I will give You thanks with all my heart;
     I will sing praises to You before the
gods.

2. I will bow down toward Your holy temple
     And give thanks to Your name for Your
lovingkindness and Your truth;
     For You have magnified Your word
according to all Your name.

3. On the day I called, You answered me;
     You made me bold with strength in my
soul.

4. All the kings of the earth will give thanks to
You, O LORD,
     When they have heard the words of
Your mouth.

5. And they will sing of the ways of the LORD,
     For great is the glory of the LORD.

6. For though the LORD is exalted,
     Yet He regards the lowly,
     But the haughty He knows from afar.

7. Though I walk in the midst of trouble, You will revive me;
  You will stretch forth Your hand against the wrath of my enemies,
  And Your right hand will save me.

8. The LORD will accomplish what concerns me;
  Your lovingkindness, O LORD, is everlasting;
  Do not forsake the works of Your hands.

Psalm 139

1. O LORD, You have searched me and known me.

2. You know when I sit down and when I rise up;
  You understand my thought from afar.

3. You scrutinize my path and my lying down,
  And are intimately acquainted with all my ways.

4. Even before there is a word on my tongue,
  Behold, O LORD, You know it all.

5. You have enclosed me behind and before,
   And laid Your hand upon me.

6. Such knowledge is too wonderful for me;
   It is too high, I cannot attain to it.

7. Where can I go from Your Spirit?
   Or where can I flee from Your presence?

8. If I ascend to heaven, You are there;
   If I make my bed in Sheol, behold, You
are there.

9. If I take the wings of the dawn,
   If I dwell in the remotest part of the sea,

10. Even there Your hand will lead me,
   And Your right hand will lay hold of
me.

11. If I say, "Surely the darkness will
overwhelm me,
   And the light around me will be night,"

12. Even the darkness is not dark to You,
   And the night is as bright as the day.
   Darkness and light are alike to You.

13. For You formed my inward parts;
    You wove me in my mother's womb.

14. I will give thanks to You, for I am fearfully
and wonderfully made;
    Wonderful are Your works,
    And my soul knows it very well.

15. My frame was not hidden from You,
    When I was made in secret,
    And skillfully wrought in the depths of
the earth;

16. Your eyes have seen my unformed
substance;
    And in Your book were all written
    The days that were ordained for me,
    When as yet there was not one of them.

17. How precious also are Your thoughts to me,
O God!
    How vast is the sum of them!

18. If I should count them, they would
outnumber the sand.
    When I awake, I am still with You.

19. O that You would slay the wicked, O God;
      Depart from me, therefore, men of
bloodshed.

20. For they speak against You wickedly,
      And Your enemies take Your name in
vain.

21. Do I not hate those who hate You, O LORD?
      And do I not loathe those who rise up
against You?

22. I hate them with the utmost hatred;
      They have become my enemies.

23. Search me, O God, and know my heart;
      Try me and know my anxious thoughts;

24. And see if there be any hurtful way in me,
      And lead me in the everlasting way.

Psalm 140

1. Rescue me, O LORD, from evil men;
      Preserve me from violent men

2. Who devise evil things in their hearts;
      They continually stir up wars.

3. They sharpen their tongues as a serpent;
    Poison of a viper is under their lips.

4. Keep me, O LORD, from the hands of the wicked;
    Preserve me from violent men
    Who have purposed to trip up my feet.

5. The proud have hidden a trap for me, and cords;
    They have spread a net by the wayside;
    They have set snares for me.

6. I said to the LORD, "You are my God;
    Give ear, O LORD, to the voice of my supplications.

7. "O GOD the Lord, the strength of my salvation,
    You have covered my head in the day of battle.

8. "Do not grant, O LORD, the desires of the wicked;
    Do not promote his evil device, that they not be exalted.

9. "As for the head of those who surround me,
     May the mischief of their lips cover
them.

10. "May burning coals fall upon them;
     May they be cast into the fire,
     Into deep pits from which they cannot
rise.

11. "May a slanderer not be established in the
earth;
     May evil hunt the violent man speedily."

12. I know that the LORD will maintain the
cause of the afflicted
     And justice for the poor.

13. Surely the righteous will give thanks to
Your name;
     The upright will dwell in Your presence.

Psalm 141

1. O LORD, I call upon You; hasten to me!
 Give ear to my voice when I call to You!

2. May my prayer be counted as incense before You;
 The lifting up of my hands as the evening offering.

3. Set a guard, O LORD, over my mouth;
 Keep watch over the door of my lips.

4. Do not incline my heart to any evil thing,
 To practice deeds of wickedness
 With men who do iniquity;
 And do not let me eat of their delicacies.

5. Let the righteous smite me in kindness and reprove me;
 It is oil upon the head;
 Do not let my head refuse it,
 For still my prayer is against their wicked deeds.

6. Their judges are thrown down by the sides of the rock,

And they hear my words, for they are pleasant.

7. As when one plows and breaks open the earth,
　　Our bones have been scattered at the mouth of Sheol.

8. For my eyes are toward You, O GOD, the Lord;
　　In You I take refuge; do not leave me defenseless.

9. Keep me from the jaws of the trap which they have set for me,
　　And from the snares of those who do iniquity.

10. Let the wicked fall into their own nets,
　　While I pass by safely.

Psalm 142

1. I cry aloud with my voice to the LORD;
    I make supplication with my voice to the
LORD.

2. I pour out my complaint before Him;
    I declare my trouble before Him.

3. When my spirit was overwhelmed within
me,
    You knew my path.
    In the way where I walk
    They have hidden a trap for me.

4. Look to the right and see;
    For there is no one who regards me;
    There is no escape for me;
    No one cares for my soul.

5. I cried out to You, O LORD;
    I said, "You are my refuge,
    My portion in the land of the living.

6. "Give heed to my cry,
    For I am brought very low;
    Deliver me from my persecutors,
    For they are too strong for me.

7. "Bring my soul out of prison,
    So that I may give thanks to Your name;
    The righteous will surround me,
    For You will deal bountifully with me."

Psalm 143

1. Hear my prayer, O LORD,
    Give ear to my supplications!
    Answer me in Your faithfulness, in Your righteousness!

2. And do not enter into judgment with Your servant,
    For in Your sight no man living is righteous.

3. For the enemy has persecuted my soul;
    He has crushed my life to the ground;
    He has made me dwell in dark places, like those who have long been dead.

4. Therefore my spirit is overwhelmed within me;
    My heart is appalled within me.

5. I remember the days of old;
   I meditate on all Your doings;
   I muse on the work of Your hands.

6. I stretch out my hands to You;
   My soul longs for You, as a parched
land.

7. Answer me quickly, O LORD, my spirit fails;
   Do not hide Your face from me,
   Or I will become like those who go
down to the pit.

8. Let me hear Your lovingkindness in the
morning;
   For I trust in You;
   Teach me the way in which I should
walk;
   For to You I lift up my soul.

9. Deliver me, O LORD, from my enemies;
   I take refuge in You.

10. Teach me to do Your will,
   For You are my God;
   Let Your good Spirit lead me on level
ground.

11. For the sake of Your name, O LORD, revive me.
　　In Your righteousness bring my soul out of trouble.

12. And in Your lovingkindness, cut off my enemies
　　And destroy all those who afflict my soul,
　　For I am Your servant.

Psalm 144

1. Blessed be the LORD, my rock,
　　Who trains my hands for war,
　　And my fingers for battle;

2. My lovingkindness and my fortress,
　　My stronghold and my deliverer,
　　My shield and He in whom I take refuge,
　　Who subdues my people under me.

3. O LORD, what is man, that You take knowledge of him?
　　Or the son of man, that You think of him?

361

4. Man is like a mere breath;
    His days are like a passing shadow.

5. Bow Your heavens, O LORD, and come down;
    Touch the mountains, that they may smoke.

6. Flash forth lightning and scatter them;
    Send out Your arrows and confuse them.

7. Stretch forth Your hand from on high;
    Rescue me and deliver me out of great waters,
    Out of the hand of aliens

8. Whose mouths speak deceit,
    And whose right hand is a right hand of falsehood.

9. I will sing a new song to You, O God;
    Upon a harp of ten strings I will sing praises to You,

10. Who gives salvation to kings,
    Who rescues David His servant from the evil sword.

11. Rescue me and deliver me out of the hand of aliens,
>Whose mouth speaks deceit
>And whose right hand is a right hand of falsehood.

12. Let our sons in their youth be as grown-up plants,
>And our daughters as corner pillars fashioned as for a palace;

13. Let our garners be full, furnishing every kind of produce,
>And our flocks bring forth thousands and ten thousands in our fields;

14. Let our cattle bear
>Without mishap and without loss,
>Let there be no outcry in our streets!

15. How blessed are the people who are so situated;
>How blessed are the people whose God is the LORD!

Psalm 145

1. I will extol You, my God, O King,
    And I will bless Your name forever and
ever.

2. Every day I will bless You,
    And I will praise Your name forever and
ever.

3. Great is the LORD, and highly to be praised,
    And His greatness is unsearchable.

4. One generation shall praise Your works to
another,
    And shall declare Your mighty acts.

5. On the glorious splendor of Your majesty
    And on Your wonderful works, I will
meditate.

6. Men shall speak of the power of Your
awesome acts,
    And I will tell of Your greatness.

7. They shall eagerly utter the memory of Your
abundant goodness

And will shout joyfully of Your righteousness.

8. The LORD is gracious and merciful;
    Slow to anger and great in lovingkindness.

9. The LORD is good to all,
    And His mercies are over all His works.

10. All Your works shall give thanks to You, O LORD,
    And Your godly ones shall bless You.

11. They shall speak of the glory of Your kingdom
    And talk of Your power;

12. To make known to the sons of men Your mighty acts
    And the glory of the majesty of Your kingdom.

13. Your kingdom is an everlasting kingdom,
    And Your dominion endures throughout all generations.

14. The LORD sustains all who fall
    And raises up all who are bowed down.

15. The eyes of all look to You,
      And You give them their food in due time.

16. You open Your hand
      And satisfy the desire of every living thing.

17. The LORD is righteous in all His ways
      And kind in all His deeds.

18. The LORD is near to all who call upon Him,
      To all who call upon Him in truth.

19. He will fulfill the desire of those who fear Him;
      He will also hear their cry and will save them.

20. The LORD keeps all who love Him,
      But all the wicked He will destroy.

21. My mouth will speak the praise of the LORD,
      And all flesh will bless His holy name forever and ever.

Psalm 146

1. Praise the LORD!
   Praise the LORD, O my soul!

2. I will praise the LORD while I live;
   I will sing praises to my God while I
have my being.

3. Do not trust in princes,
   In mortal man, in whom there is no
salvation.

4. His spirit departs, he returns to the earth;
   In that very day his thoughts perish.

5. How blessed is he whose help is the God of
Jacob,
   Whose hope is in the LORD his God,

6. Who made heaven and earth,
   The sea and all that is in them;
   Who keeps faith forever;

7. Who executes justice for the oppressed;
   Who gives food to the hungry.
   The LORD sets the prisoners free.

8. The LORD opens the eyes of the blind;
    The LORD raises up those who are
bowed down;
    The LORD loves the righteous;

9. The LORD protects the strangers;
    He supports the fatherless and the
widow,
    But He thwarts the way of the wicked.

10. The LORD will reign forever,
    Your God, O Zion, to all generations.
    Praise the LORD!

Psalm 147

1. Praise the LORD!
    For it is good to sing praises to our God;
    For it is pleasant and praise is becoming.

2. The LORD builds up Jerusalem;
    He gathers the outcasts of Israel.

3. He heals the brokenhearted
    And binds up their wounds.

4. He counts the number of the stars;
    He gives names to all of them.

5. Great is our Lord and abundant in strength;
    His understanding is infinite.

6. The LORD supports the afflicted;
    He brings down the wicked to the
ground.

7. Sing to the LORD with thanksgiving;
    Sing praises to our God on the lyre,

8. Who covers the heavens with clouds,
    Who provides rain for the earth,
    Who makes grass to grow on the
mountains.

9. He gives to the beast its food,
    And to the young ravens which cry.

10. He does not delight in the strength of the
horse;
    He does not take pleasure in the legs of a
man.

11. The LORD favors those who fear Him,
    Those who wait for His lovingkindness.

12. Praise the LORD, O Jerusalem!
    Praise your God, O Zion!

13. For He has strengthened the bars of your gates;
    He has blessed your sons within you.

14. He makes peace in your borders;
    He satisfies you with the finest of the wheat.

15. He sends forth His command to the earth;
    His word runs very swiftly.

16. He gives snow like wool;
    He scatters the frost like ashes.

17. He casts forth His ice as fragments;
    Who can stand before His cold?

18. He sends forth His word and melts them;
    He causes His wind to blow and the waters to flow.

19. He declares His words to Jacob,
    His statutes and His ordinances to Israel.

20. He has not dealt thus with any nation;
    And as for His ordinances, they have not

known them.
Praise the LORD!

Psalm 148

1. Praise the LORD!
Praise the LORD from the heavens;
Praise Him in the heights!

2. Praise Him, all His angels;
Praise Him, all His hosts!

3. Praise Him, sun and moon;
Praise Him, all stars of light!

4. Praise Him, highest heavens,
And the waters that are above the
heavens!

5. Let them praise the name of the LORD,
For He commanded and they were
created.

6. He has also established them forever and
ever;
He has made a decree which will not
pass away.

7. Praise the LORD from the earth,
   Sea monsters and all deeps;

8. Fire and hail, snow and clouds;
   Stormy wind, fulfilling His word;

9. Mountains and all hills;
   Fruit trees and all cedars;

10. Beasts and all cattle;
    Creeping things and winged fowl;

11. Kings of the earth and all peoples;
    Princes and all judges of the earth;

12. Both young men and virgins;
    Old men and children.

13. Let them praise the name of the LORD,
    For His name alone is exalted;
    His glory is above earth and heaven.

14. And He has lifted up a horn for His people,
    Praise for all His godly ones;
    Even for the sons of Israel, a people near
to Him.
    Praise the LORD!

Psalm 149

1. Praise the LORD!
    Sing to the LORD a new song,
    And His praise in the congregation of
the godly ones.

2. Let Israel be glad in his Maker;
    Let the sons of Zion rejoice in their King.

3. Let them praise His name with dancing;
    Let them sing praises to Him with
timbrel and lyre.

4. For the LORD takes pleasure in His people;
    He will beautify the afflicted ones with
salvation.

5. Let the godly ones exult in glory;
    Let them sing for joy on their beds.

6. Let the high praises of God be in their mouth,
    And a two-edged sword in their hand,

7. To execute vengeance on the nations
    And punishment on the peoples,

8. To bind their kings with chains
    And their nobles with fetters of iron,

9. To execute on them the judgment written;
　　This is an honor for all His godly ones.
　　Praise the LORD!

Psalm 150

1. Praise the LORD!
　　Praise God in His sanctuary;
　　Praise Him in His mighty expanse.

2. Praise Him for His mighty deeds;
　　Praise Him according to His excellent
greatness.

3. Praise Him with trumpet sound;
　　Praise Him with harp and lyre.

4. Praise Him with timbrel and dancing;
　　Praise Him with stringed instruments
and pipe.

5. Praise Him with loud cymbals;
　　Praise Him with resounding cymbals.

6. Let everything that has breath praise the
LORD.
　　Praise the LORD!

entirely JESUS
entirelyjesus.com

Praise the Lord!

Made in the USA
Coppell, TX
21 October 2021